Stop Over-Spending

24 Little Tools to Help Stop Your Big Spending Habits

Jennifer Chase

Financial Coach & Professional Organizer

JENNIFER CHASE

DEDICATION

To my husband, Dan. We have been through hell and back
emotionally, spiritually, physically and financially.
I have made us go broke. I have broken us.
You encouraged me to change my money habits, my
spending habits, and encouraged me to success.
I love you crazy for that.
I'm so excited for you.

CONTENTS

No Chapter Titles.
No Page Numbers.
No Descriptions.
Nothing listed here.
YOU HAVE TO READ IT AND DO IT!

ACKNOWLEDGMENTS

To Dave Ramsey and his team at Ramsey Solutions. I know you run a business and I know you teach about finances, but you also changed my life and changed my family tree. Thank you.

INTRODUCTION:
LET ME SUM IT UP FOR YOU

I SUCK AT MONEY. I do. I own it. I suck at it. It's like an alcoholic coming into the light and acknowledging that there is a problem. "Hello, my name is Jennifer, I have a problem with money!"

I have a spending problem, it's called "I want it now, so I'm getting it now" disease. Have you ever heard of it? It is intense! I also have another disease called "Budget? What the hell is a budget?" Have you ever lived that disease out loud? It's powerful and awesome too! These money diseases made me go broke.

I ROCK AT MONEY. I do. Really! Even after hearing everything I just wrote before, I really rock at money! I love it! I own it! I have it! I got my junk together and got my finances in order too. I no longer over-spend money I haven't earned yet. I no longer over-indulge with money I already did earn. I live what I call a "Frugi Life". A life filled with balance, maturity, simplicity and only the things I truly love.

I am no longer childish in my behaviors concerning money. I grew up about my money. I got serious and intentional about my money. I even became a Financial Coach. Go figure? Me? Someone who sucks at money and someone who rocks at money.

You picked up this book because you are serious about getting serious about your over-spending. Like me, you suck at money, suck at finances, suck at a budget. But also like me, you are ready to rock it too! You totally can do this!

Oh yes, here we are. Another book telling you how to change spending habits, stop over-spending and all the world will be right, filled with sunshine, unicorns and rainbows, all while becoming a millionaire overnight. Um, NO. This is not that book. Although, I am crazy about unicorns!

Here's why this book is different.

I am going to offer you 24 tools, habits really, that have helped me in the past and help me on a daily basis today to stop over-spending. I am going to write them each down for you, spell it out for you, be honest with you and kick your butt into gear helping you get intentional about changing your big spending habits.

And within each tool, I'm going to ask you QUESTIONS to answer along the way so we can dig down deep, go back so we can go forward.

I am also going to offer you SCRIPTS that will help you in daily decisions, your relationships, your home and work life, and pushy sales people. You will have the script ready to answer anyone about your decision about how you will be spending your money.

Some of the questions I will be asking you are the same exact questions I have asked myself and continue to ask.

"Why do I spend so much money?"

"Why can't I stop over-spending?"

"Why can't I save any money?"

"Why are we always fighting about money?"

Good questions! Going deep! We will answer them together. We will work through this junk together.

I am so ready to get started. I want to help you stop over-spending. It's my passion, it's my goal, it's my life. I've been there and I've been here. And if you happen to see unicorns with the rainbows along the way, you might need another book that explains why that is so wrong in real life. Let's get started!

CHILDHOOD, IT SCREWS US UP

My childhood consisted of good times, great family vacations, nice houses, a car when I turned sixteen, a good church family, a Mom and Dad who did their best to keep food on the table, clothes on our butts and a trip to Disneyland once in a while. It was a pretty good childhood. BUT, my childhood screwed me up financially!

My parents went bankrupt when I was a teenager. You would think I would learn from this fiasco? No, no I did not.

What I learned in childhood was that we could spend until our hearts desire was met! Spend money on groceries, spend money on clothes, spend money to go on vacations and fun trips, spend money on stuff we wanted and stuff we didn't even want. Just spend away! We were happy, right? No, no we were not.

My parents separated, we lost our home, our cars, we lost income, we lost time together, we lost so much money to debt. Maybe not in that order, but when you lose everything, does the order really matter?

What I also learned in childhood, was that my Mom would spend and my Dad would try and recover. Very typical case of enabling. Can you relate? My Dad worked two jobs for the past thirty years of my life, just to make ends meet and pay off debt. My Mom worked also, mostly to pay off debt.

I grew up watching my parents over-spend and then try and re-group and re-coupe. So, I brought all that money junk into my marriage and into my adult life. What a nice gift for those who love me and live with me. Insert sarcastic tone here.

Everything I learned as a child, good and bad, I brought into my relationship with my husband. I would spend and spend and expect him to recover the losses or find a way to pay for everything.

"Figure it out! It's not my problem!" I have actually said those words out loud. Or, I would go to work part-time or full-time to help pay off debt. No, I worked to have money to spend any way I wanted.

Just like me, everything you learned as a child about money, good and bad, you have brought with you into adulthood and into your relationships. Childhood screws us up.

"My Mom was so sweet, she did everything for me." Wonderful, I'm not saying Mom isn't sweet. Then why are you broke?

"My Dad did the best he could." Great! Dad is the best! Then why are you over-spending and not good with money?

"I don't want to talk negative about my parents because that's not respectful."
Then you will not be honest with yourself and honest about your childhood. You might as well put the book down now and go find one that makes you feel all special inside and doesn't hurt your cozy feelings. This book is certainly going to piss you off.

You want to know what is not respectful? Not preparing a child to become an adult, fully functioning, working, living on their own. I was not prepared to be an adult. And well into my forties, even today, my parents still treat me like a child with the silent treatment, the punishments, the verbal assaults and not being allowed to be a part of my family unless I live exactly the way they want me to. Can anyone else relate to that drama?

I have learned from my family drama. I have learned that I want to change my family tree. I do not want to act like my parents, especially in finances and how I love my children. I want to train my child up, so that he can grow up. I want to teach my sons about finances, so that there will be no need to have emotional strings attached.

I want my boys to be adults after childhood. And I would love for them to re-write this chapter and change the title: "Childhood, it built me up."

Maybe my parents thought I was strong? A social butterfly who would find her way? "She's capable of working and paying bills?"

"We had to figure it out ourselves, so why bother teaching her about a budget, balancing a checkbook, or what to do with all this cash?"

Maybe my parents weren't taught either by their parents and so on and so on? Just like you?

The way I got healthy about money as an adult, was being honest about my money in my childhood.

There were many wonderful positives about my life growing up. But, there are some real deep scars that I have on my heart and my soul that were burned into me in childhood that I dragged on into adulthood. I believe Psychologists call this "baggage"?

As I live my life by the motto "Go Big or Go Home", I brought not only a few bags but an entire dump truck of emotional crap into adulthood, into my marriage and into my parenting. And, at the time of this writing, my husband still loves me! Although, he did make me dump the truck of baggage years ago.

How you were raised as a child in money, determines how you live as an adult in money. I do not know what your home-life was like growing up. Wonderful? Blissful? Horrible? Evil? We all have a story. We all have a history. We all have a childhood.

Let's just admit right now, that most of our parents did not know what the hell they were doing with money. From bank accounts to new credit cards and second mortgages, they were learning how to deal with money while we were growing up.

How we were raised is vital to understanding why we over-spend. Sometimes, I have found myself over-spending because of my childhood and the junk that happened to me. I try and soothe that little girl who just longs for peace and just wants to be loved. If I can't experience that from parents that reject me now, I should just spend money on this amazing jacket that looks completely even more amazing on me! Right?

Or, if my family went on vacations that I long for and miss those special times together, I should just go on a caribbean cruise on this credit card to feel wonderful again to remember the good old days?

Or, my Mom doesn't even like me and my Dad didn't choose me. I should just shop at the mall all weekend to make me feel better about not being loved. I will love myself by spending money and maybe my things will make me feel better?

Or, your parents did everything for you. Picked out your clothes, chose what you ate, attended every honor roll party for you and you were perfect. You should spend money on yourself because honestly, you deserve it.

See how all of our childhoods, different, the same, honest, can relate to how we spend money? It does not matter how you were raised, how much money you were raised with, which parent sucked more at money, or whether or not you feel like it was good or bad. Our childhood determines how we spend today. Our emotions, our memories, our brains, our actions, our comfort zones, all work together to determine how we spend money.

Let's dive on in deep. Take some time and write answers to these questions. Really ponder on them. Think back to your childhood. You will be amazed how this little exercise opens, releases and throws out some "baggage".

Did you have a good childhood?
Why or why not?

Were you taught positive things about money such as
Budgeting? Saving? Investing?

What did your Mom teach you about money?

What did your Dad teach you about money?

What did the person who raised you teach you about money?

I went to a college that had no problem putting me thousands of dollars into debt before I even took one class. Borrowing money for school loans that would later place me in such hardship to pay my bills and make a living was the norm. And that was a Private school! Why the hell did I take out those student loans? Because that's what everyone did! I was taught in my childhood that everyone took out school loans to pay for college. I was taught as a child that school loans are "good debt" and a "necessary evil" to earning a degree.

I was also taught as a child that taking out a loan for a house is just the way we do it. Then, take out a second loan on that same house to put in a pool, finish the basement, get a new kitchen and more toys. After all, it's what we do.

Then, let's run out and get a new car! Sign for a car loan or even worse a car lease! Whoo-Hoo! After all, I have to drive something nice with leather to get to work to pay off all the debt I've racked up in school loans, mortgages, and did I mention the credit cards?

I was taught as a kid that credit cards work to get you what you want and when you want it-NOW! No worries, no interest until you can't pay the minimum and then we tack on about 29% interest, so really we pay double for that TV, lobster dinner, Mexico vacation, water heater that went out last week, or that one perfect wedding dress and did that marriage last?

You know what all this taught me to be in adulthood? Broke. Stressed out. Maxed out.

What were you taught as a child about student loans, mortgages, car loans/leases, and credit cards?

Do you think all that teaching was right? Or wrong?

The way I grew up living was paycheck-to-paycheck, I just didn't know at the time that's the way my parents were getting it all done.

I also grew up on loans, leases, mortgages, second mortgages, and credit cards. I just didn't really understand the power of all those debt items.

I grew up not wanting for anything, really. I always had a roof over my head, a car to drive to work and school, always had money to spend and went to college. But now I realize it wasn't real. It was all based on debt and extended living. We were living a lifestyle we couldn't afford. We were broke.

Then came my life. As a single woman, I was horrible at money. As a married woman, I was even worse. I just kept over-spending each time a paycheck came in and then was always waiting for the rescue. Insert childhood here.

Replaying in my mind the lessons in childhood did not serve me well into my mind as an adult. In childhood, we went bankrupt and lost everything. In my adulthood, I did the same. Funny how childhood affects us, even in our twenties, thirties, forties, and so on if we allow.

I decided along the way, I no longer wanted my childhood to continue to affect my adult living. I wanted to love my life, physically, emotionally and financially. I wanted to live in financial freedom! But I would need to release some childhood junk in order to love my life.

I learned some negative things about money as a kid. I needed to deal with them.

For certain, I learned to spend and over-spend until there is nothing left in the checking account. I learned to not save, because there was always a fun trip to take or fun night out. I learned I would need to be rescued, that meant I would need to find an enabler as a partner that would just let me spend. I wanted to unlearn these bad ideas.

Name three **NEGATIVE** *things you learned about money in your childhood that you emotionally carried with you into adulthood:*

Name three **POSITIVE** *things you learned about money in your childhood that you emotionally carried with you into adulthood:*

Positive things I learned about money in my childhood that I emotionally carried with me into adulthood are truly just money facts.

Money can give me a wonderful lifestyle that I lead with a beautiful home, gorgeous cars, amazing vacations, family time together, starting and growing businesses.

Money gives me the ability to walk away from a job I hate and a relationship that is not healthy.

Money I earn gives me a fantastic income to feed, clothe and care for my family.

Money gives me options and freedom. Money gives me peace.

I don't remember feeling that way about money growing up. Whenever finances or money were brought up, I remember it was a fight or an argument about over-spending again. I remember sleeping in my Uncle's closet when we had lost our home and I had lost my bedroom. But I'm not certain I really understood that we didn't have a HOUSING problem, we had a MONEY problem.

In childhood, I did not understand how important money was. It was just a negative subject, the elephant in the room, something we actually kept in the closet.

Money should have been taught, earned and respected. I should have grown to understand how money is a powerful tool for me to learn how to use, multiply, bless others and give me and my family a wonderful life.

Instead, I went deeply into debt beginning early in my twenties and beyond. I went bankrupt because I over-spent my way into debt that I could not pay. I was never taught good things about the power of money and the importance it brings to my life. Instead, I had to learn the hard way.

Hopefully, you have not made all of the stupid decisions I have made about money. Just so you know, if there is a bad way to handle money, I have done it. Maybe even twice and many times over. Stupid does not cover the full scale of my epic money failures. Nothing illegal, never stole it. See, there's a positive. And now back to my screwed up childhood.

I know my parents were doing what they thought was right. But it was wrong. I know my parents tried to give me the best childhood they wanted for me. But it wasn't best. I know my parents got better with money over time, but not until their 60's. I know my parents. And I know I am a lot like them.

I have to take ownership of my childhood, and my adulthood. They are weaved together, wrapped so lightly, occasionally bumping into one another. And I need to recognize when my childhood comes whispering or screaming into my adulthood to take hold, cause chaos, give me false emotions and fears, drawing me down paths of debt and into a history that has already been written.

Years ago, my parents introduced my husband and I to a life-changing book called "The Total Money Makeover" by Dave Ramsey. It's fantastic irony that the very parents who taught me horrible things about money, also gave me the best insight and training about money through this book.

Dave Ramsey lays it all out on the line. He shows you how to do a budget, pay off debt and live a life of financial freedom. Get his book today!

Childhood, it screws us up. Acknowledging the truth about the things we went through and learned about money as a young child will help us to be really great with money as a grown-up. My childhood, it really screwed me up. But, as crazy as it was, it's still mine. I own it. I lived it. I survived it. I actually even love parts of it. And now, in adulthood, I am so excited to get old and live a great life with money.

One of the ways we can control our bad habits of bad spending is to understand how our childhood negatively and positively affected us financially. It is okay to admit it all. Place it at the feet of who is responsible and then let that stay there. Now, it is your responsibility to stop over-spending, start saving, live a life in financial freedom.

I am going to give you tools to help you change your bad habits. You will find that these tools are useful in helping you curb your over-spending, over-eating, over-indulging, over-parenting, over-anything.

I want to help you gain control of your entire life. Unless you are willing to make little drastic changes, this is not going to work.

I had to get crazy! I had to get mad! I had to get going! I had to work! I had to get ferocious! I had to find my fire inside! I had to get lioness! I had to get radical in my thoughts and feelings about money! So, I did.

My Mantra:

My childhood screwed me up. But, it's my history and my past. I have the capability and responsibility to write a new history and my future. I will be intentional about getting educated, changing my habits and moving forward in my adulthood about love, life, and my money.

Write your own Mantra about your childhood:

TOOL #1

SUCK IT UP, BUTTERCUP!

SHE SETS ME STRAIGHT AGAIN
SHE SAYS, "SUCK IT UP, BUTTERCUP.
YOU'VE GOT WORK TO DO.
PULL YOUR BIG GIRL PANTS ON 'CAUSE YOU
GOT BIG DREAMS WAITING FOR YOU."
-ELLA REID

The power to tell ourselves the word "No" is an amazing gift. The power to tell our children, "No" takes a tough spirit and is a wonderful gift we give our children.

The word "No" is tough-talk for someone who is over-spending, over-debting, over-indulging, running up credit cards, not living within a budget, heading towards bankruptcy and heading out to the next fun event tonight.

Go ahead and make more excuses if you need, but you are broke. You need to make some sacrifices and have some seasons of intentional living regarding your money.

I have read many books and listened to many speakers give me great ideas, great insight, great motivational speeches in order to help me master my money. But the one thing, the one area I had to start with in my verbal and emotional control was to suck it up and learn how to use the word "No".

Daily-Do: Suck it up, Buttercup and tell myself NO today so I will be able to say YES tomorrow.

I had to learn the **SCRIPTS** to tell myself and my children:

"No, we don't have the money for that right now".

"No, that is not in the budget this month."

"No, I am not buying that."

"No, I am not spending money on that today."

"No, I am not signing up for that credit card offer, ever. Thank you."

I had to suck it up and be honest with myself that I had a problem and I was out-of-control in my over-spending.

I was selfish.

I was childish.

I was depressed.

I was fearful.

I was dishonest.

I was acting entitled.

Princess Buttercup.

I was spending money I had, spending money I didn't have. I was working to pay for the next fix. I had the head knowledge, but no desire to take it to heart.

I made money only to wake up and realize that every penny had to be written to a bill collector or lender. It was time to just suck it up and say, "No." I was done living this way.

I had that mirror moment, you know the one where you look at yourself in the mirror and realize you don't know who you are?

I looked at myself and said out loud, "Suck it up, Buttercup! It is time to deny yourself a few things."

Frequent trips to Starbucks, frequent trips to Cosco, frequent trips to fast food joints, frequent trips to my favorite retail stores, frequent trips to the spa, frequent shopping online. It was time to deny myself a few things.

I made little drastic changes in my life and it helped me control and curb my over-spending immediately! I love Starbucks, but instead of twice a day, I enjoy a delicious coffee there about twice a month now.

I no longer have a membership to Cosco. That's a personal choice I made so I would not enter there while I could not control my spending in that amazing wear house of goodies!

I started eating healthier, skipping the fast food and enjoying the slow cooker. As a family, we love fast food. There is wonderful, deliciousness of grease to be eaten out there! But, instead of 3 nights a week eating out, we eat out about 3 nights a month now. Our kids love it more too, because it is more like a special treat and not a regular occasion.

I stopped walking into my favorite retail stores. I used to frequent a beautiful boutique in town once a month spending over $100 easily, and I now walk in about once a year. Don't worry, that small business does just fine without me and they sell merchandise online too!

Oh, I love the spa! Massage and hair color and nails. Did you know that can cost $600 per month. Trust me, I do! I went back to coloring my hair from a box, massage quarterly, not monthly and my nails look great short and clean at home.

My online shopping is shut down, only attached to a budget. Clothes, home goods, and other items we can purchase for a lower price online, that is when I'm online to shop. But I do not click on to shop every day. That's just a habit I developed and continue to develop.

Suck it up, Buttercup! I made this mess and now I am going to clean it up! I start with "No" so one day, I can say, "Yes!".

I learned to say, "No" to some very basic, little things. No to daily coffee, no to big wear house shopping, no to daily eating fast food, no to monthly retail spending, no to online shopping every day. I just started there. And you know what happened? I loved it! I felt more in control. I felt like an adult. I felt more freedom in saying, "No" than using a continual "yes!".

These little radical changes didn't destroy me, didn't negatively affect me. I learned to love my coffee and creamer I make fresh at home every morning. I don't miss my big shopping trips in a wear house. Maybe just the free food samples? I learned how to cook really great dinners! My family actually eats them! We often cook together, have nice meals together and even clean up the mess together! I haven't missed out on a thing. Any sale online I did not click on, came around again the next week anyway. Just because it says, "Last chance!" does not really mean it.

I had plenty of more chances to get a good price on an item I needed, when I had the money to pay for it.

Such a simple word with such great power. Saying NO to myself and my children have helped us all learn lessons in delayed gratification, saving money, and choosing to spend wisely. It has all been worth it.

This month, I got my hair colored by a master stylist in town. It looks amazing! I have said NO for years and this month, I saved up money and said YES!

Yesterday, I got my nails done at a local nail salon. For years, I said NO, but yesterday with cash, I said YES!

All week we said NO to the boys for eating out, so tonight we say YES to order a pizza! Greasy deliciousness!

I have specifically chosen to have seasons of "NO" so that I can now have seasons full of "YES".

Suck it up, Buttercup! It is time to say NO now, so you can say YES later.

What are three ways you spend money that you can say **NO** *to yourself & your children right now. How much money will you save each week, each month changing each habit?*

MONEY MANTRA: I will say NO today, so I can say YES tomorrow.

TOOL #2

STOP LYING, START TRUTHING

IT'S JUST TIME TO PAY THE PRICE
    NOT LISTENING TO ADVICE
    DECIDING IN YOUR YOUTH
    ON THE POLICY OF TRUTH.
                    -DEPECHE MODE

But it's so easy to lie! Lying to ourselves, lying to others, lying to the lender, lying to the boss, lying to friends, lying to our spouse, lying is just easy! Especially when you are good at it!

I have lied about my age, my weight, my bankruptcy, my money issues, the state of my marriage. I have lied about everything. It doesn't make me a horrible human being, it just makes me have to work harder to tell the truth. Lying is a character trait, and I have full power and authority to change it.

After learning a lifetime of lying, I wanted to begin another lifetime of truth telling. I wanted to learn how to be honest, in everything!

I learned that lying just kept placing the truth off for a bit. It didn't matter the lie, I felt that the truth hurt too much, so I would rather stay in the lie to look good, sound good, feel good and act good. I was lying about lying!

My entire life was a lie. Think about that one! I was lying to myself, my children, my husband, my neighbors, my co-workers and supervisors. I was lying to lenders when they would call. I lied to friends, family and anyone asking about our money issues. It was easy to lie. It is not easy to tell the truth when you have developed a bad character.

I needed to learn how to stop the lying and start telling the truth about my money. I needed to change my character.

I've become pretty in-your-face about debt, about credit cards, about bad spending habits. But, it took me awhile to get here.

I've become pretty unstoppable in learning how to develop better character traits in my heart, my mind, my soul and then living it out loud based on a foundation of truth.

Whether it is to save face, look better in front of others, impress people or whether you have a character weakness like me, you can find your way home. In truth!

I learned how to stop lying and it started in my heart and in my home. A change of heart can help you practice in your home. I keep getting up when I hit the ground. When I fail, I own it. When my children fail, we deal with it. When my tongue begins to rule, I question it like it is a living thing. I actually speak to my own tongue! I tame it!

In the Christian faith, there is a section of the Bible from the book of Proverbs, Chapter 6, verses 16-19. You have got to listen to this!

It describes what God hates. Hates! Not dislikes, not that it bugs him a little, He hates it!

"There are six things that God hates, yes even seven that are an abomination to Him."

Abomination? I'm going to go with that means this is bad, really bad.

"A proud heart, **a lying tongue**, hands that shed innocent blood, a heart that devises wicked plans, feet that run to evil, a false witness who speaks lies, and one who spreads lies among others."

Lying tongue is listed among hands that shed innocent blood! Even evil! It's that serious! It's more than serious, God hates a lying tongue. Are you getting this whole "hates" thing?

I hated that I had a lying tongue. I wanted to have a tongue of truth. I wanted to be a woman of honor, honesty, good character. I wanted to have self-control and tame my tongue.

You will find that you need to be truthful in all things. Be truthful about your relationships, your work, your home life and your money. When you are truthful in all things, you will find that everything becomes reality. Everything becomes the real, the real truth, and then you can honestly deal with it.

When you learn to have a character trait of being honest, it affects all areas of your life, especially your finances. Being truthful allows for us to take charge, take ownership and lead in all areas of our finances.

Are you being honest about your money? No one wants to be honest that they are horrible with money. It's not like I was shouting on Facebook posts letting everyone know that I was completely failing at finances and standing on my rooftop with a neon sign flashing "I'm a failure" while yelling "Yep! I suck at money and I lie about it too!"

No, my honest change was honestly subtle. It was a heart change. It was a mind change. It was a soul change. It was a habits change. It was a tamed tongue change. And people noticed.

When I tamed my tongue, I stopped the lies and I noticed that it allowed others around me in my life to get honest and real about their truth issues too.

When I tamed my tongue, I stopped yelling, stopped arguing, stopped the negative and I noticed that my husband and children did the same.

When I tamed my tongue, I got honest about my money problems and my bad spending habits. I noticed that when I spoke the truth, I was able to better control my spending. My tamed tongue was able to help me tame the spending beast.

I became myself in truth. I was honest about my money and I became honest about everything. It was a natural progression into changing my character trait from liar to honest heart. I moved into living a life of truth.

What are you lying about today? It can be about money or anything else in your life. Are you willing to be honest about it?

That's how I tamed my tongue. I got honest about it. I started speaking truth every day, in the little things and then the big things. Practice. Practice. Practice. Because I was practicing how to tell the truth, it became so easy to say it. It was awesome! It was freeing! It was truthing!

How will you learn to tame your tongue? Put one thing into practice today.

I think after I speak. I listen after saying a word. I have an opinion for everything and sometimes I come off as a know-it-all! Shocker!

So my **DAILY-DO** is to think BEFORE I speak, listen BEFORE I say one word. Keep my opinion to myself often, because not everyone wants it. I do not know everything. I want to enjoy the company of my husband, my children, my friends and family and if I am going to do that, I will tame my tongue.

Daily, I practice listening, looking into someone's eyes and confirming they have been heard! I practice keeping my mouth shut. I practice softening my blows. I practice taming my tongue every day and with every truth spoken, I celebrate building a better character trait that I have worked so hard for!

My tongue can break down, hurt, destroy, and act like a sword. So I choose to take my tongue and speak truth, light, and love into the lives of people every day. I draw my sword when needed. Practice this daily.

SCRIPTS that have helped me in my journey to stop lying and start truthing that I speak out loud and say to myself include:

"Stop talking. Listen first, then speak."

"I don't want to be a liar."

"I am changing my character right now."

"Where is this false word coming from? I want to speak the truth."

"I am taming my tongue today."

"God hates my lying tongue."

I tell the truth about my money. When people ask, I tell them. My husband and I went bankrupt. We over-spent our entire marriage. We both brought childhood junk into our marriage. But we educated ourselves, we changed our hearts and we changed our lives.

Now, we live debt-free, we live on a budget, we make killer incomes that we get to keep because we owe no one. We tell the truth about our spending and we get to say YES!

It's an amazing life and that is the truth!

MONEY MANTRA: I will tame my tongue to speak the truth in everything, including my finances.

TOOL #3

UNPLUG, UNSUBSCRIBE, UNDO

WHO DO YOU NEED?
WHO DO YOU LOVE?
WHEN YOU COME UNDONE.
-DURAN DURAN

Many of you are scared, I mean flat out fearful of unplugging, unsubscribing, and undoing. What if you actually don't see something? What if you miss out on that sale that will never come around again, ever?! What if that breaking news gets away from you and you're the last one to know?! What if I don't post about it? What if I don't respond to that email in 1.4 seconds? What if we don't schedule ourselves or aren't busy to the max? Imagine, what if?

I don't have to imagine the what if. I have made unplugging, unsubscribing and undoing an art form in my life and in my home.

I was afraid at first. It was different. It was change. That can be scary.

But, once I began to make little steps like unplugging the phone and letting it die, unsubscribing from emails and magazines, while undoing some over-scheduling I had wrapped my life around, it became easier to do it all!

What does it mean to unplug? Unplugging is all about disconnecting. That includes disconnecting your mind and body from computer, phone, work, projects, over-booked schedules.

Unplugging is about disengaging from your normal activities. What are your normal activities? Work, carpool to sports every day, constant communication tools, t.v., spending money, shopping and entertainment. It's all a part of our normal day, our normal activities. Anyone tired of the normal?

Kids sports are out of control. This activity has become a part of your normal activity. Practices every night of the week, games every weekend, and don't get me started on the traveling teams. Do you even realize how much money you are wasting on sports for your kids?

Disconnecting from sports is a great way to stop over-spending. If sports is your entire schedule and you haven't had dinner at home together as a family in years, its time to sever this connection.

As the Mom of five boys, don't write me or call me screaming your complaint about the importance of sports and the benefits of sports and how your kid is going all the way! Complaining to me that I just don't understand is ridiculous. Did you read the part about the 5 boys? Sports have always been a part of our family life. However, in my home, we have some Unplugging rules regarding sports.

SPORTS SCRIPTS.

"No one in the Chase home is allowed to play two sports at the same time."

"No one is allowed to be a part of a traveling team. We will not be spending that type of money on you unless it is your college degree."

"No one is allowed to have sports interfere in their homework and school work."

"No one in the Chase home is required to play a sport."

"Mommy & Daddy will NOT be sitting at every single game, in fact, just be pleasantly surprised if we show up for a couple of them."

"Sunday's are family day's. You need to be home on Sunday's to get ready for your week, have dinner as a family and relax."

"But Jen, you don't understand the importance of sports! You are killing your sons dreams! You are a horrible Mom! Kids need sports! Your sons could have been sports stars! You are missing out on all that traveling and your child will not be a complete human being or a well-rounded individual unless he is playing a sport! If you don't attend every single practice or game, your sons will never know you love them!"

It's soccer people! It's a ball! It's just a sport. It is not LIFE! Get over yourself and get the facts. And if you think that this is love, then I need to write a whole other book on that pathetic way of living and thinking.

I have two sons living out of our home and three still growing up at home. Our older boys each played sports, they each did not go to college to play sports. They have an amazing life without sports. They have wonderful relationships and a bright future without sports. Both our grown sons work, go to school, live on their own, make their own decisions, pay their own bills and it's funny, because they both know they are loved , live great lives, have amazing experiences, without playing sports!

They don't ask for a thing. And they don't cry over sports. It was their choice not to play sports anymore. It was their choice to focus on their education and career instead. It was their choice to stop wasting so much time on sports and start living their successful lives. They have grown into really great young men and I am so proud of them!

All five of my boys have played sports since a very young age, and three of my boys who still live at home continue to play sports occasionally or they choose to play instruments or take wonderful art classes and spend time with other fun activities.

However, MY entire life and MY schedule does not evolve around MY children, or their sports, or their activities. I miss a lot and I do not feel guilty about it. In fact, I feel great about it!

Sports and activities have costs. We trade our family time to focus on one kid. That has a cost to other children in the family. We trade our work time that produces income to sit watching a game or racing to an activity. We trade our hard earned money, it has a cost to our checkbook and savings. We trade our weekends to go sit watching games. That has a cost from relaxing and connecting.

Full sport schedules, terrible refs, unruly parents and even fights between players and parents. I don't miss out on much. And my sons don't enjoy the screaming parents or coaches. Or coaches screaming at refs or parents screaming at the coaches and refs or even parents yelling at them. Sportsmanship left sports a long time ago. When being a good sport comes back to the game, maybe I will too.

So much of youth sports is about earning that scholarship, being better than the other kid and don't get me started on the parent problems. Sports are no longer about just having fun, being a part of a team and learning about good sportsmanship. Sports became stressful and I just don't make time for that.

How much are you spending on sports every month?

Add it all up. Include costs such as gas, car upkeep, airfare, snacks, dinner and lunches out, team fees, uniforms, Coaches gift, and your time. It all has a worth, a value, a cost.

I am giving you permission to unplug from sports. If you are over-spending money each month, it may be because of the costs of sports that you or your children are involved in. Allow yourself to undo the sports and activities schedules and participation.

"Who do you need? Who do you love? When you come undone." Duran Duran is one of my favorite childhood bands. Come Undone is one of my favorite songs! Using their words, I am asking you the same questions? When you unplug, who do you need and who do you love? And, are you making the best decisions for them?

What and who are you spending all this money for? For someone else to pay attention? For someone else's love? For someone's approval? For the hope of maybe getting a scholarship? For a great Facebook post? Shut it down, turn it off, be unplugged!

Besides sports, what are some other ways you can unplug and stop over-spending?

One of the ways I can truly unplug is by unsubscribing from email alerts, retail store emails, online presence everywhere, blogs and magazines.

Now, as a Blogger, did I really just ask you to unsubscribe from blogs? Yep! That's how serious I am about this! Choose your TOP 5 Blogs that you love, and the rest, Unsubscribe from them right now! We are clearing out, we are unplugging, we are organizing and we are disengaging from this entangled web of information all the time!

I have a **DAILY DO** of Unsubscribing. It's amazing how my email addresses end up subscribed to things, companies, information, stores I have never set foot into. And yet, here it is, almost daily, I receive an email about the latest and greatest sweater I must have for the amazing discounted price of…..I DON'T CARE! CHECK UNSUBSCRIBE!

I actually get giddy about unsubscribing every day! It has become part of my organizing therapy! Clicking on the Unsubscribe word in emails is so freeing! It's my little way of saying, "Goodbye, good luck to you!" and "Hello, Freedom!"

I utilize e-mails as part of my businesses. I serve others through email. I often communicate through emails. I give information through emails. What is so great about my emails? I am able to offer a service to those in need and those who want my services. I also offer someone the ability to Unsubscribe from receiving my information, my target marketing. It is so freeing to use it as a business tool and freeing to offer a client a way out and a way to unplug.

Besides offering a service to you, what am I also doing when I send you an email? I am soliciting you for money. What the??? No, really??? You want my money???

Yes! That sums it up. I am looking for you to spend more money so I can grow my business. It is pretty simple and that knowledge is pretty much already out there.

Do you think maybe that's what email marketing is about? Do you think maybe emails could be helping you find great deals while helping you over-spend? Do you think all those posts and pictures are designed to sell you something? Spend here! Click here! It's so easy! You don't want to miss this!

You are over-spending online. I know that you are, because I did! I was spending there! Clicking there! Spending and clicking everywhere! It was so easy! And I just didn't want to miss out on that sale!

And then, the next day, there would be another email or another posting telling me about the newest sale, better than the previous sale and it would never return, ever!

Hook, line, sinker. Drowning in debt.
I unplug, I unsubscribe, I undo to stop over-spending.

The undoing is actually harder than I thought. We sign up for a membership, or sign up for that crazy sport schedule, or sign up to work all those extra hours, or sign up to volunteer, or subscribe for every magazine, or subscribe for all the emails for discounts, subscribe to every blog, every newsletter, every app, and on and on it goes.

The undoing can take time. It is a clear thought out plan. It is a clear intention. It is a clear focus and actions.

What I learned about the undoing is that it often occurs in the undoing of our marriage, our family, our career. There is a natural undoing in our relationships when we change our focus. There is a natural undoing in our tragedies and broken places. We learn to stop the madness and slow down, and breathe and hope that everyone is okay, that everyone is going to live.

We naturally undo when everything falls apart. And in those moments, we wish we had spent more time, more energy, more focus on one another, or caring for ourselves, to be prepared for this moment. This sadness. This grief. This end.

We naturally unplug, unsubscribe, undo when the worst is upon us. When the world is falling apart. When grief has taken hold.

I learned to live my life unplugged, unsubscribed and undone. Who do you need? Who do you love? When you come undone. I love my home, I love my schedule, I love our lives together.

I focus on my boys now. I focus on my marriage now. I care for myself now. I focus on my work that I love now. I spend time with friends I love now. I travel now. I read now. I relax now. I refuse to wait until the next tragedy, next horrible phone call, next news story, next hospital stay. I will never regret these moments of unplugging, unsubscribing and undoing so I can plug in, submit to and do the things I love and be with the people I am crazy about!

When your child is in the hospital, you don't care what time practice is. When your husband is hurt in a car accident, you don't care what retail store is having a sale. When you can't pay your bills, you should not be caring about the latest and greatest gadget available online.

Live your life prepared for whatever comes. Live your life balanced and that includes your checkbook. Live your life free!

When you practice this lifestyle, your scripts will become your own and you will offer them freely. Living disconnected for a bit, sever the un-meaningful connections, remove obstacles and relax by disengaging. I love this life, I long for you to live it.

MONEY MANTRA: I will unplug, unsubscribe, and undo from anything keeping me and my family from having close relationships, a fun and peaceful home, and a wonderful life we choose.

TOOL #4

STOP COMPETING, START CONTENTING

'CAUSE INSIDE I REALIZE THAT I'M THE
ONE CONFUSED. I DON'T KNOW WHAT'S
WORTH FIGHTING FOR OR WHY I HAVE TO
SCREAM. I DON'T KNOW WHY I INSTIGATE
BUT NOW I HAVE SOME CLARITY, I'LL
NEVER BE ALL-RIGHT.
SO I'M BREAKING THE HABIT TONIGHT.
                              -LINKIN PARK

Think about it. Everything in our life is a competition. Let me break it down for you.

Where we live. How big our house is. What clothes our kids wear. What car we drive. What activities our kids are involved in. Where we attend school. Where our kids attend school. Where we go to church. Where we work. How much money we make. How much money we give. Where we eat. Where we vacation. Who we date. Who we marry. Our hair, nails and shoes. How many followers we have. How many likes we get. It is all a competition. I am tired just typing this crap!

Who doesn't love a little friendly competition? I do! I love to compete! In a sport, in business, in good wines! I love to watch good competition too! I love watching others compete and win! But this book is about real life and real money. The real competition is within ourselves.

Some of us are still acting like children when it comes to competition. Trying to keep up with the Jones's and most of us don't have a relationship with the Jones's anymore. We are continually trying to keep up or show up the neighbors, the boss, friends, family and everyone around us. We are always trying to win! But do you even know what the trophy is?

If you want to stop over-spending, stop competing. You are competing against the world and against yourself. You are spending money to stay in competition with a world around you that doesn't even care about you and by the way, the world hands out trophies to everyone now just for showing up.

When you stop competing, you will save money, save time, save energy, save face and become a better person. You will love your life when you learn to not give a damn what someone else thinks about you! You need to read the book by author Rachel Cruze, "Love

Your Life, Not Theirs."

This has been one of the most freeing, fulfilling decisions I made in my life. While becoming debt-free and changing my money habits, I let go of the world. I let go of what my neighbors thought, what my friends might think, how my family might feel or what my online presence looked like. I let it go. And by not caring what others thought about me or my lifestyle, I was able to create one that I love!

The definition of the word "compete" is a verb. It's always in action. It's always moving in motion. It's always competing about everything.

"Take part in a contest."

"Strive to gain or win something by defeating or establishing superiority over others who are trying to do the same."

Wow! That is an awesome way to live, right? Being in a contest all the time? Trying to establish superiority? That sounds truly exhausting and miserable.

I compete in business, I compete in my personal life. And sometimes I win, sometimes I fail and sometimes I just let the other gal win. Because I don't care. I don't need to be holding the trophy! I don't need the recognition, I don't need a hi-five and I certainly don't need a win to feel like a winner!

I don't have to be the best at everything, and my children don't need to be either.

I love being my best at the things I am best at. I don't need to be the best at your best. You do your thing, I'll do mine. There is room for everyone. There is space for all of us to win. There is plenty of money out there to go around.

I used to be horrible at this. Really bad. I was always competing. And then I learned more and allowed into my heart this one word: "CONTENT".

The definition of "content" is an adjective meaning "in a state of peaceful happiness". Or content can be a verb meaning to "accept as adequate despite wanting more or better."

WOW! A state of peaceful happiness sounds way better than a state of contesting or defeating. I choose to live a life of contentment. That does not mean my life is boring, without meaning or purpose, and it certainly does not mean my life is not without wonder and amazement! I just choose to be content.

Have you ever been content?

Are you content now in your life?

Where does your discontentment come from?

I lived the first 40 years of my life not being content. In fact, I was always looking for more. More in my home, more in my marriage, more in my closet, more in my career, more, more, more.

I was never satisfied. It was never enough. I realized, I wasn't happy with me. This is how you get content. Learn to LOVE YOURSELF. Once I dove in deep to dealing with my issues, my hangups, my childhood, I learned to love myself and love all my great traits. I love all that I have to offer my husband, my children, my friends, my team, my world. I love me! Yes, there are some traits I do not like so much. That is a whole other therapy session. But I am learning, practicing and getting educated about how to get better at that junk.

DAILY DO: If I want to be truly content and not compete in everything, I need to learn how to be GRATEFUL daily. The other way you get content is to be grateful. If you are not grateful for you, your health, your home, your family, your work and all that has been given to you, you will never be content. And you will always over-spend.

Loving you and being grateful are the only ways you will ever be content. You must let this love and gratefulness sink into your soul and let it spread throughout you. Oozing out of you!

When the discontenting thoughts and fear creeps in, here are a few of my **SCRIPTS:**

"Do I really need that right now? Where is that thought coming from?"

"Why am I feeling so discontent right now? What is going on in my heart?"

"I love my home just the way it is."

"I love my marriage and I am married to a great guy."

"I am so thankful that my family and my children are healthy today!"

"I love my car. It is paid off and gets me to where I need to go just fine."

"Thank you for work and for the ability to earn money! Let's do this!"

See how you can change your thoughts and your actions by having some scripts questioning your discontentment and readiness to be grateful?

When we are content and grateful for the things we already have, it changes our spending habits on the things we don't yet have. Gratefulness and contentment bring fullness that lowers the feeling of emptiness.

Once again, practice. Practice being content in the moment. Practice being grateful in the moment. This is not a simple answer of "just be happy!", "just feel content", or "just feel grateful!" and everything will be wonderful and fabulous every day! No, it takes intentional living and practice.

If you want to stop over-spending, stop competing in every area of your life and start being content and grateful in every area of your life. OOZING.

MONEY MANTRA: I want to live today in a state of peaceful happiness, not in a constant state of over-spending competition. I'm happy, I'm grateful, I love who I am and I love my life just the way it is in this moment.

TOOL #5

RELAX

WE WERE KILLIN' TIME
WE WERE YOUNG AND RESTLESS
WE NEEDED TO UNWIND
—BRYAN ADAMS

All I did was write the word "Relax" and you went into a tailspin. Didn't you? You may have even said out loud, "Don't tell me to relax, lady!" But, relaxing is exactly what you need to do in this moment. You want to stop over-spending.

What in the world does RELAXING have to do with stopping my over-spending habits? I'm so glad you asked!

If you are always on the go-go-go, you are most likely also on the spend-spend-spend.

If your daily habits include having to be somewhere, having to get something done, having to be with someone, you are spending. But if your daily habits make room for relaxing a bit, you most likely are not spending in that moment. Let me explain.

I love to relax at home. I can be a home-body every day if needed. I love to relax by reading books, watching chic-flicks, writing, taking a nap, taking a bubble bath.

I love to relax by having conversations with my sons, I love to write down my goals and to-do list. That is actually relaxing to me! I also love to get organized! Getting organized in my home, my office, my finances is so relaxing and makes me feel great! Because getting organized takes the stress out of it all. Listening to my favorite Podcasts or Radio Shows while I relax is perfect! Get's my mind off of spending too.

In all of that relaxing, I didn't spend one penny. Not one dime. Not one dollar. Nothing! No spending. No over-spending. Relaxing feels great and feels even better on the budget!

We all have that friend, maybe it's you? Always on the go! Have to drop off the kids, pick up the kids. Have to meet up with a friend. Have to go get lunch. Have to go get dinner. Have to work. Have to work overtime. Have to volunteer. Have to lead all the Bible Studies. Have to get groceries. Have to get that thing for the house. Have to get to practice. Have to go to the game. Have to be somewhere tonight and have to somewhere in the morning. Have to buy a new outfit. Have to get here, have to get there.

Nothing listed above is bad. Nothing listed above is a terrible thing to do. Many of them need to get done, I mean, someone has to get the groceries! That can be a major first-world catastrophe in our home! But does it always have to be her? Does it always have to be you? Does it have to be today? Right now? Is it a daily go-go-go?

Do you know how to relax? Relaxing is one of the best ways I changed my bad spending habits. I learned to relax and learned to not spend money every single day.

Today is a Thursday. Thursday is one of my days I choose to not spend any money. It's before the weekend, it's in the work week and it's usually my least scheduled busiest day.

So, I choose Thursday's to not spend money and certainly not over-spend any money. If something comes up, I just use the **SCRIPT:** "Can it wait until tomorrow?" "Can it wait until payday?" "I am not spending money today." Mostly, it can wait. When I refrain and hold off from making a purchase, often I don't really need it or I change my mind to not purchase it the next day, or the next payday.

Thursday's, I get to relax! Often, I don't

even leave the house! Just between you and me, I am still in my jammies! Soft and cozy, writing a book. It costs me nothing!

DAILY DO: I woke up and made my coffee and poured my creamer. Relax! Enjoy! Later in the morning, I made myself a green smoothie with Almond Milk, banana, blueberries, and Spirulina. Getting my folic acid and vitamins in today! Relax! Enjoy! Just finished a load of towels. Don't have to get it done this weekend! Relax! Enjoy! It's lunch time. Made myself a tuna sandwich. Sitting at my dining table, getting ready to listen to my favorite Dave Ramsey Radio Show. Relax! Enjoy! It's all free! And I listen to Dave daily! Anyway I can, I listen to Dave. His show is always a part of my Daily Do. And back to writing my book for you. A couple chapters complete. Did not cost me any money to write today. Planning dinner, only using what is in my fridge or freezer. It's smelling delicious in the crockpot. So far, nothing spent today.

List 5 ways you love to relax? Then, put them on your schedule.

Is there a day you could choose to not spend

Things come up. I get it. Life happens. Sometimes, we are committed! We are NOT going to spend any money today! And then a kid needs supplies for a school project in an hour and then the dog runs out of food and then a medical bill pops up. It happens. Don't take it as the "whole day is ruined" mentality. Just know that you are within a budget and will only buy those things absolutely necessary today. Everything else can wait. No over-spending. Now, back to relaxing.

Relaxing does cost money sometimes. I put relaxing in my budget for the things I love to do in order to relax and take care of myself. For instance, I love to get a massage at least every couple months. Put it in the budget! Then you don't feel guilty about it and it feels amazing! I love to travel. Especially to a beach or a mountain filled with snow. That is relaxing to me. I love to travel, so we put it in the budget. I also love to go for sushi lunch at one of our local favorites here in Colorado. Put it in the budget! I can relax and enjoy that wonderful lunch time. I love to get my nails done, and my hair colored. Those things are relaxing and such a treat to me! I put it in the budget! Relaxing needs to be put in your life, put on your schedule and placed within your monthly finances.

Today, I am going to read a book in bed relaxing, and I am going to write some goals for my business. It will feel great checking that off the to-do list and then I can relax even more. Less Stress = More Relaxing.

I absolutely love the definitions of RELAX: "Make or become less tense or anxious." Doesn't that sound wonderful? Or how about this definition? "Rest or engage in an enjoyable activity." Yes! Choose me!
And yet another, "Make less firm or tight." Pretty certain that is about my body. Thank you massage!

I put relaxation on my calendar every week. By relaxing at home or outside of my home, I get better at spending wisely. Because I am not stressed out to the max or so tired I can't see straight! I am in control of my thoughts and my emotions and I am in control of my spending. When I have intentionally made room and space in my life to relax a bit, it makes room and space in my life peaceful, fun, loving and an adventure.

Over-spending is about hating your life

and your schedule. You over-spend because you are never really home or present in the moment, because you always have to be somewhere. Your busyness is helping you go into debt. Busyness with no relaxing or enjoying is just busy.

Relaxing does not mean you are lazy or not accomplishing anything. Relaxing is doing something, it's doing what you need right now. It is one of the best accomplishments! Relax. Enjoy.

The boys are all starting to come home from school now. I'm going to shut it down for a bit. Listen to their stories, spend some time together over a snack. I am going to be intentional about looking into their eyes and just relaxing together.

Learn to become less tense and anxious about everything. You will spend less.

Learn to rest and engage in enjoyable activities you enjoy doing. You will spend less.

Learn to make your body less firm and tight. You will spend less. I promise you! Relax.

MONEY MANTRA: If I learn to relax, I will learn to stop over-spending. Relaxing daily gives me more control over my money.

TOOL #6

STOP WHINING,
START WORKING

YOU WON'T SEE ME CRY
NEVER LET 'EM SEE YOU DOWN
GOTTA SMILE WHILE YOU'RE HURTIN'
WHISTLE WHILE YOU WORK IT
                    -KATY TIZ

I could start here by saying, just whistle. Stop your whining and start your whistling. But you know what, Snow White, that just didn't cut it. You have to stop whining and you gotta work! You can whistle while you work, but you gotta work your ass off!

I work my ass off! Do you? If I don't have one job, I have four. You too? If we need extra income, I go earn it. If I ever found myself starting to whine about not having enough money for a trip, or not enough in savings, or not enough to pay the bills, I worked. It's what I've always done.

But, I found that I was part of the

problem as to why we didn't have money for that trip, or that money in savings, or enough to pay the bills that month. The problem was me and my over-spending. Insert knife here. Right next to the heart.

Working my ass off and nothing to show for it, except maybe a great ass! My butt looked great, but it was tired! I was tired of always having to owe someone else or owe the bank. I was tired of every penny being spent before it was earned and then once earned I over-spent because I was working so hard and felt entitled to spend it, I mean, I earned it! Do you see the hamster on the wheel spinning? I got tired of being tired. And then, I got mad.

If you make the decision to Stop Over-Spending, if you want to live a life that is debt-free, if you are ready for financial freedom and earning income for you, then get mad, and take this one line, and write it on your heart, mind, and soul.

YOU GOTTA WORK YOUR ASS OFF!

I have worked for over 45 companies in my 45 years of living. My jobs over the years have included, Babysitter, Movie Theatre Ticket-Taker, Flight Attendant, Radio Host, TSA Officer, Retail Manager, Professional Organizer, Store Owner. I have worked so many jobs for so many companies and for myself. All my jobs have been a bit different, yet all the same. I had to work!

Each job required that I show up on time. Can you believe that?

Each job required I actually get something done while at work.
Crazy? Right?

And every single job required that I give great Customer Service. I mean, the gall! Then, they would pay me.

I learned to work by working. I learned to write by working. I learned how to be great at business through working. I learned how to curb my spending while working. I learned how to not spend anything while working.

I have so many failures at work. And I have so many successes at work. I have learned from them all and I wouldn't trade it. I had horrible bosses, I had the best bosses! I had terrible co-workers and I have worked along side some of my best friends today! I have hired and fired. I have learned the keys to success, the in's and the out's. I worked!

I have gotten up in the middle of the night to report to work at 4:00am. I have worked nights, I have worked mids. I have worked long days and part-time too!

Many of you are showing up to a job you

hate. You are working with people you cannot stand. You are stuck and you whine about it constantly. You are fully capable to changing your job and your income. It starts with you stopping the out-of-control spending.

Or, you aren't working at all, yet you have all the time in the world to whine about your financial problems. Just so you know, people who whine to me about their money problems and sit at home doing nothing about it, are not my people. I'm not your girl. I will tell you to go get a job or start a home business and get it done! Stop whining and start working!

Many of you who have picked up this book, and I thank you very much, have a spending problem and you have a working problem. I can say that because I had a spending problem attached to an entitled working problem. I was working, therefore I felt I could spend it all! Thus, the problem.

While I have been writing you, I just Unsubscribed my email from another retail store! Boom! Feels good! Now, back to my broke over-worked ass.

Many of you might be working and working really hard right now! Whoo Hoo! So proud of you! But it's not enough? And the bills still don't ALL get paid? And you're tired? And you are tired of being tired! And you are getting mad! And you are wondering where in the hell does all the money go? My hand is up! I know this one! I know this answer! You over-spend. And if it's not you, it's your family and you let it happen. And now you know. You are welcome.

Right now, in this moment you need to make some decisions. I will ask the questions, you answer honestly, and then put your answers into motion. I will guide you, give you some tips, but ultimately this is all you, baby!

Regarding money, what do you whine about most? Can't pay the bills? Can't get ahead?

Are you working right now? Why not?

How could you bring more income into your financial life? Get a job? Start a side-hustle?

Are you whining about your money? What are some ways you could stop doing that?

One of the ways I stopped whining about our financial situation was to take responsibility for it. I had to really look at MY spending habits, MY money issues, MY relationship with money. I could not control Dan or our kids to a point. They all needed to make their own responsibility decisions. I had to make mine.

Once I began to focus on my money-junk, so did my husband, so did my kids. They could see my passion, my fire for paying off debt, not over-spending, sticking to a budget each paycheck. I spoke it out loud! Dan felt respected when I didn't continually spend us into an oblivion, and the kids respected our decisions to respect our money. They are growing up with that respect.

WHINING SCRIPTS: "You can whine about it all you want, but I am not purchasing that today."

"I'm sorry, that is not in the budget this week, let's try to put it into the budget next time."

"Whining does no good. Let's work for it."

"I am not going to whine about this anymore, I am going to solve the problem."

I still say these scripts out loud all the time! Recently, a water heater went out in our home. Now, we did have another water heater still working pretty good, however, with five people living here, after using the dish washer and laundry and a couple showers, we were finished! And I mean freezing cold water finished! In Colorado! In the Winter!

I was annoyed! And it was usually MOM who got the cold shower! So, I whined about it a little bit. Then I kept whining about it.

One final freezing cold shower, I said to myself, "I am going to stop whining about this and fix the problem." So, we saved up the money to purchase a new, bigger water heater. It took us two pay periods, sacrificing eating out, sacrificing some entertainment and extra spending, but we made it! Then, my husband called a great plumber for the install. We paid cash for it all! It felt wonderful! And the hot water flows in this house! In fact, I will be showering this morning in it and basking in the hot water glory!

DAILY DO. What do I do daily that stops the whining in my head and in my heart? I need to control my thought patterns. I need to control my fears. I need to control my tongue. I need to control my spending.

Daily, I work on the contentment and gratefulness piece. Daily, I work on the budgeting piece. Daily, I work on controlling my tongue to speak positive and speak life. Daily, I work. I put into action and solve problems by earning income or getting tasks completed.

I have been whining in my head about being a Vendor with my Frugi Organizer business here in Colorado at a wonderful event for Moms. I have fears about it. It's hard to put yourself out there. Out there can be rejection, hurt feelings and lost sales. But my whining has been crippling me to make a decision. I stopped my internal whining last night. I signed up to be a Vendor!

I spoke about all the positive that could happen, I spoke life and growth into my business, into my head and my heart. I finally made the decision and I'm going to work at this event this Spring. So excited to move past the fears and move into motion!

I also paid cash from my business checking account to be a Vendor. So, I start the day paid-in-full. No debt. And it was such a reasonable price to be a Vendor, all I will need is to find two new clients or three new Consultants and the event will pay for itself. I can recover the cost of the event quickly. That's just a great business decision and I am not whining about that!

I have loved writing about this tool for you. I hope this one sinks in deep and you put it all into action starting today!

MONEY MANTRA: I will take responsibility to control and stop my whining. I will start working and winning!

TOOL #7

DO-IT-YOURSELF

```
        I WON'T GIVE UP
  NO, I WON'T GIVE IN UNTIL I REACH
THE END AND THEN I'LL START AGAIN.
 I WANT TO TRY EVERYTHING ALTHOUGH
           I COULD FAIL.
                          - SHAKIRA
```

One of my favorite spaces in my home is my mudroom. When we first built our home, there were 5 doors in this one space. One entry door from the garage, which we use the most living in Colorado weather. Then there was a door to the basement. Then there was a door to a storage closet. Then another door to laundry area, then another door next to the other two doors for basement and closet. Did you keep up? Doors everywhere! Did that drive you nuts? It drove me nuts for years!

So one day, my husband came home to doors and walls gone! I had two of my sons join me in putting on gloves and eye protective gear, grab a big hammer, turned off the electric and knocked it all out. It was beautiful and messy! For months!

One year later we have finished this beautiful space by doing almost everything on our own. It was a Do-It-Yourself project for sure! And worth it all!

My mudroom is my favorite drop zone ever! My amazing husband made me barn doors that roll from a huge opening space. They are gorgeous! Then my husband helped pick out new lighting and installed the lights. Stunning! Then he built a wall unit with locker style cubbies for all of us, so we all have a drop area for our stuff. I painted the room a bright white and decorated with only things I love. It's the best! AND, we paid cash for everything as we went along the project, so no debt. My mudroom feels even better in it fully paid for.

The only thing my husband and I knew we needed an expert on was the flooring and electrical. We had a tile contractor complete the entire floor area and backsplash behind sink and counter. It is beautiful! Paid cash for that work and we appreciated the saved time and energy having someone else do that work for us. We also had an electrician install the electrical wiring and switch plates for the new light area, locker area and inside the closet. We saved money by installing the lights ourselves, but the wiring was tricky and we needed an expert! The electrician also made me a special switch to be able to turn the lights off in the basement from the top of the stairs, instead of having to walk downstairs to the basement to turn them off if the boys had forgotten. It feels like a dream! I am so thankful every time I turn on and off my lights from the areas I need. So worth the cost!

Most of our work was completed Do-It-Yourself style. If you are always paying someone to fix or make or design or install something for you, you are over-spending.

When you do a lot of the work yourself, you save money and can save up money to pay an expert to complete work that is beyond your capability and time.

Learning how to Do-It-Yourself can save you tons of money! Watch any video on You-Tube, shows on HGTV channels and many local contractor websites and you just might find how easy it is to install lighting, or tear down a wall, or paint a room. And, when you put your own blood, sweat and tears into it, watch how you love it even more! You gotta have some skin in the game, not just always paying someone else.

Learning something new is also good for your soul. Using your brain and your body in new ways is psychologically positive to your life. It gets you moving, it gets you active, it gets you sharing your work on media sites everywhere, touting "Hey! Look at what I did! Can you believe it?"

A great way to stop over-spending for any task, for any project, for any re-model is to have a budget. Have an idea of what you can afford. Have an idea of how much cash you need to save or budget each week to complete. Have an idea that this will take some time! Don't be in a hurry. When you hurry, you over-spend.

Our Mudroom project took exactly one year. We did it exactly the way we wanted it completed by taking our time, preparing to spend a budget, and only spend cash. Taking our time also helped us make the best decisions.

Stop spending on services. If you add up how much you spend on services every month, you will find a lot of extra money doing it yourself from time-to-time.

Add it all up! All the services. Drive-thru coffee, dry cleaning and laundry service, maid service, milk delivery, and on and on. Services can get expensive. Plus, add the Cable and internet, phone services, utilities, basic services we need daily. When you add it all up, you are spending a lot of money for services you might be able to do yourself sometimes or all the time.

Last year, we stopped our milk delivery service. We found that the milk available from our local market was cheaper and since our boys go through about five gallons per week, we needed to watch our milk costs. So now, I watch the local coupons and get our milk cheaper when I grocery shop instead of delivery service.

I rarely drive-thru for a coffee. I know, I know! It's amazing! That deep roasted coffee with foamy milk with a sprinkle of cinnamon on top of the whip cream! I totally get it! But I save hundred of dollars every year not driving thru for coffee. Also, I enjoy it more when we do drive-thru for a specialty coffee. It's a real treat for me and my family! I can make a great coffee or cappuccino at home anytime for about fifty cents, saving 8 bucks!

Services I do pay for and I am willing to put in my budget are dry-cleaning pick-up and drop-off service as well as a Maid service bi-weekly. Being debt free, and busy, I love these services! My husband is a Pilot. His uniform shirts need to look nice, and we are actually paid back a portion of dry cleaning costs through his company. When I try and iron his shirts, I can do a pretty good job, but they do not look professionally pressed. It's best that we have a service do his shirts.

I have special fabric items in my wardrobe that can only be dry cleaned or I ruin them. I also need to look nice when I make presentations, speeches, and appear on media. Those services have a huge value to me and they save me time and less gas costs running errands.

Maid service is a huge help to me and my family! We complete a lot of chores every day. We do a lot of the cleaning and upkeep, but it's nice to have a cleaning service come in and complete a deeper clean in my bathrooms and kitchen a couple times per month. I love having someone else vacuum too! It's such a blessing to support local women in business and be blessed by their work!

Just like doing a major remodel, you may need professionals to help you complete a task that is necessary. But, don't burst the budget! I would love to have daily maid service. That is not in my budget!

DAILY DO: So, we clean our home and do chores daily while having maid service do a deep clean Bi-Weekly.

I would love to have daily dry-cleaning service, but that can be a budget-buster for sure!

DAILY DO: So, we have pick-up and drop-off service two times per week and on other days in-between, we iron ourselves or wear clothing that does not need a dry-clean, saving tons of money!

What are 3 things I could do myself around the house to get a project completed?

What are the projects I need to hire a professional to complete and save up money to pay cash for their services?

What are 3 services I could cut back on or do myself more often?

What are services I absolutely need and will put in my budget every week?

Now, I find myself asking these questions for every little and big thing.

SCRIPT: Is this something I can get done myself? Or should I really hire a professional for this one?

SCRIPT: Is this a service I really need? Or, could I do this myself to save money?

When I ask myself these SCRIPTS, I find that I tend not to over-spend on services and projects. I feel amazing when I can learn something new, complete it myself and I feel amazing have someone else help me too! But, I've made better choices, smarter choices about what I can do myself and what a professional needs to help me with.

Do-It-Yourself. Just another tool to help you stop over-spending. And, if you can't do-it-yourself, be sure to put a budget in place and pay with cash for services and the stuff you need.

MONEY MANTRA: I can do this myself. If I don't know how, I am going to learn and teach myself. If I absolutely need someone's help, I'm paying cash.

TOOL #8

STOP USING CREDIT CARDS, START USING CASH

WHAT DO YOU SAY TO TAKING CHANCES?
WHAT DO YOU SAY TO JUMPING OFF THE
EDGE, NEVER KNOWING IF THERE'S SOLID
GROUND BELOW, A HAND TO HOLD, A HAND
TO PLAY? WHAT DO YOU SAY?
-CELINE DION

"Everyone uses credit cards."

"You need a credit card to build credit."

"I need a credit card to earn points and free miles!"

"I have to keep a credit card for emergencies." "How do you rent a car without a credit card?"

I have heard it all. I have lived it all. I have also gone broke and lost a business because of credit cards.

I bought the lies too! I was taught that EVERYONE uses credit cards. It's just what we do. The truth is, not everyone uses credit cards and they have a wonderful life.

I was taught the lie that credit is good. I was taught that you need to build a good credit score by going into debt with a credit card so you can continue to go into debt by borrowing money you don't have and may never make in your lifetime. Stop and think about it. Does that even make sense?

I was taught the lie that earning miles, earning points and then earning free stuff is the way to go! Just use the credit card so easily to purchase everything and then you earn miles and points! Whoops! I have to pay off everything I use it for? Silly me. But I earned a flight to Hawaii! But I earned a free microwave! It was not FREE. It was paid for, by you and you paying interest. The truth is, nothing a credit card company offers you is ever FREE. Get out of that thinking process. It is a lie. The truth is, wealth is never built by borrowing on credit cards.

The truth is, we over-spend with credit cards and then rack up bills that are overwhelming.

Many of us live as slaves to our credit cards for years, even our entire lives. Meaning, you go to work every day to pay a credit card or lender.

Many of us choose to live our lives according to keeping a good credit score number. Meaning, you stay in debt and pay off debt continually.

You live your life according to some number!?!?! Stop and think about it. Does that even make sense?

DAILY DO: I choose to never live according to that number ever again. I choose to never live as a slave to a lender ever again. I choose to never live my life according to someone's debt-to-income ratio over me. I choose to work and keep the money I have earned. I choose to never use a credit card ever again.

I have not used a credit card in over eight years. I have never owned a credit card in that time frame. I have used a debit card attached to my bank accounts. I have used cash. That's it!

"But, what do you do in an emergency?" I use my savings. If I don't have the money in cash, I make payment arrangement to the hospital or entity. I pay them cash I earn and save. But, I don't go into debt.

"But, how do you rent a car?" I rent very easily all over the country using my debit card. I just have to verify which company allows me to use a debit card and while I drive their vehicle around, they place a "hold" of about $500 or more on my bank account. I just have to remember to place some additional funds in my account to cover the rental and my vacation spending. That's all. It's quite simple.

It is also amazing! It is so freeing! The freedom of owning my life! The freedom from using credit cards and not owing debt on them! My life is not determined nor financed by some credit card company telling me what to pay, when to pay, what interest to pay and how long I will be paying it. UGH! That is not a life!

Aren't you tired of paying credit cards? And fees? And interest?

Aren't you tired of paying every month on something you can't even remember you purchased?

Aren't you tired of being a slave, working for the master of card companies?

Well, aren't you?

Cut up the cards, close the accounts, take chances. I took a chance on not using credit cards. I took the chance of not having a credit score. I took the chance of not knowing what solid ground was below. I jumped on in and I love it!

A tool you absolutely need in taming your spending monster is to get rid of credit cards. You must stop using credit cards. Have I made myself clear? I am telling you the answer to your money problems and you are arguing in your head with me about this action. Because you have been trained to believe the lies. You are brainwashed. You are coming out of a fog into the light of truth. This tool is vital to use. Stop using credit cards, start using cash and you will stop over-spending.

Go get the scissors! The really crazy big ones! Now, go get the credit cards. ALL OF THEM! The retail stores, the gas cards, the airline miles, the home furnishing cards, the remodeling cards, the appliance cards, the car repair cards, the medical expenses cards, all of them! CUT THEM UP! Into tiny little pieces and place them into three different trash bags and then place them out in the trash bins.

I am not talking about Debit Cards attached to your cash in your bank accounts. I am only referring to Credit Cards that are not cash based. The ones that destroy your life in debt.

You will stop running up charges you can't afford. You will stop going further into debt and down a further hole. You will stop over-spending and live a budget lifestyle in peace.

You don't need them! You need to not need them! You need to not be needed by them!

Here come more excuses! I can hear them!

"But, I need a credit card and credit history to rent an apartment?" No, you don't. You might not be able to rent from a certain property or company, but there are many reputable property owners and companies that do not require a credit history. You might have to get creative.

"But, I'll save 25% off all my purchases at that retail store!" No, you won't. You will over-spend on purchases at that retail store thinking you are saving 25% and end up owing more since the average interest on a retail store credit card is 29%. Do the math.

"But, I'll earn a free trip to see my grandmother or that amazing vacation!" No, you can't. Once again, do the math on what you are spending in interest payments alone on an airline credit card with an average percentage of 29% in interest every month. Have you seen how cheap it is to fly these days? Pay cash! Enjoy Grandma's house even more knowing the trip is paid for! Enjoy your vacation on miles that are paid for!

Have your scripts ready for combat! It's war out there to get you!

SCRIPT: "No, thank you. I only pay cash for my purchases. I don't need a credit card. Thank you anyway."

Retail Associate then says, "But you can make a payment any time to pay if off, you could even come into the store and pay it with cash."

SCRIPT: "No, I don't want to have to pay off a credit card or have to make a payment every month. That's why I pay cash at the time of purchase, thanks."

SCRIPT: "I save money every day by not using a credit card. Thank you."

SCRIPT: "But if something goes wrong and I can't pay it one month, then I'm paying triple the original amount of today's purchase. That would be silly of me! No thanks!"

Cut 'em up! Let 'em go! I want to hear those scissors! Chainsaws if necessary! Take a picture and tweet it to me @FrugiOrganizer or post on media at Frugi Organizer! I love it!

Do you even know how many credit cards you have open on your credit? Do you know how much you owe on all of them? Do you know how much interest you are paying on each one? These are answers that you need to answer today. It will be empowering and healing. Knowledge is power and dealing with it is healing.

List each credit card name or lender with amount due and interest for each one.

Now, list them in order from least amount due first to the greatest amount due last. It is not about interest, it's about amount due.

Now, begin to pay off the first one with the least amount due. This is how you get out of debt. Write it here and make a plan to keep paying off each one. Give it a goal or an end-date! Least to greatest. Watch the progress you make!

MONEY MANTRA: Cash is King. Credit Cards do not own me. If I don't have the cash, I don't buy it.

TOOL #9

STAY HOME

LET THE RAIN WASH AWAY ALL THE
PAIN OF YESTERDAY AND THOUGH MY
KINGDOM AWAITS AND THEY'VE
FORGIVEN MY MISTAKES,
I'M COMING HOME, I'M COMING HOME,
TELL THE WORLD I'M COMING HOME.
                    -SKYLAR GREY

Stay home. You purchased a book that just told you to stay home. Yes, can you tell I am not a trained psychologist or educated master financial planner? But, sometimes I do sound brilliant! I'm real and I am honest! If you have an over-spending problem, you need to learn to stay home once in a while and maybe more often.

"Stay home, Jen? Really? That's stupid and ridiculous." **MY RESPONSE SCRIPT:** Actually, what is stupid and ridiculous is your over-spending, over-analyzing, over-charging, over-debting, and over-tweeting about it!

SCRIPT: Stupid and ridiculous is how I used to live my life, spending out-of-control. Smart and reasonable is how I live my entire life now.

And, only after making some serious financial mistakes that I want to help you from making or experiencing. Ever.

I learned this little gem years ago while paying off debt and living broke. Stay home. I had to get intentional about every penny, every dollar if I was ever going to pay off debt and save money. I learned to stay home. I learned to stop over-spending and learned self-control and self-respect. I learned new habits. And then kept learning.

What are five things you could do at home today?

DAILY DO: I make a To-Do List for every day. That includes staying home. I can stay home and complete many tasks. And, often, I just ask myself, "Do I really need to leave the house today?"

"What can I get accomplished at home, and not spend any money today?"

"Can this wait until tomorrow or another day I am driving by?"

Five things I am getting done at home today are:

1. Laundry. The boys and I have completed six loads of laundry already! And folded! Boom!

2. Complete two chapters in this book to stay on target for completion date. Almost finished!

3. Deep clean my kitchen. It needs it. I need it. From dishes to counters to floors, cleaning needs to be completed today. This one will take a while!

4. Watching Hallmark and chick-flick movies. Okay, maybe this is not getting something done, but it's awesome!

5. Going for a walk down to the creek with my family. It's an easy walk from our home and it is a beautiful day here in Colorado. Sunshine is out, we need to get out in it! Staying home does not mean staying in the house. You can find activities right outside your doors for free.

What are three things you could do right outside your doors today for free?

There are many days throughout the month that I choose not to leave my home, but instead, I relax in it, clean it, get some projects completed, get work done and write a book at home! I take a walk, I ride a bike, walk over to a friends house. I love my home!

For many years now, I have work meetings, networking events, and team training sessions in my home so I don't have to leave! So sneaky! And income producing!

Often, when you don't leave the house, you don't over-spend. Often, when I am out running errands, running around, I am running up my expenses!

I stay home now and then. I can work from home, I can even get shopping completed from home, either online or by delivery. There is so much we can get accomplished or not get anything completed that day at all!

You know how I want you to relax, stop competing, stop whining and do things yourself. Well, staying home allows you all those possibilities!

When you choose one day to not spend anything, you can also choose to just stay home on that day. It's a win-win!

When I stay home, I can get my entire home organized again, especially my places in my space I love. Being organized is a true passion of mine. I've built an entire business serving others and have trained others to have a business to serve others by helping them get organized. Organization is my thing!

And, it's my therapy. I work through my head junk when I organize my pantry. I work through my mommy and daddy issues when I scrub clean floors I just picked up. I work through my self-doubt and fears when I organize my mudroom into order. That's how I deal with stuff. By organizing my stuff.

If you choose to stay at home, get organized. It is the best gift to give yourself and your loved ones.

When you stay at home, deal with stuff. Either clean it out, throw it out or get it in order. Stuff should not rule your home, and staying home allows you to rule it again. This includes emotional stuff and mental stuff. Sometimes, when we are emotional or mentally not healthy, we should stay home. It's best for everyone if we stay home and deal with our stuff. Home can be the best place to relax, get healthy, get things in order and take a break from the world. Learn to love home and stay home.

MONEY MANTRA: I need to stay home today so I can control my money and just enjoy being here.

TOOL #10

STOP DIETING, START LIVING

WHEN YOU LOVE LIFE, LOVE LIFE,
IT'S BEAUTIFUL.
WHEN YOU LOVE LIFE, YOUR LIFE,
IS BEAUTIFUL.
-NATALIE TAYLOR

What does dieting have to do with stopping the over-spending? Dieting is expensive, time consuming and not a lifestyle. Dieting should be a starting point to lose weight, not a way to spend your entire life trying to lose weight.

Many of us have made dieting a lifelong journey. It's time to stop dieting and start living.

This is the part where I have to tell you that I am not a Doctor, I am not a Dietician, I am not a Physical Therapist, nor am I a Personal Trainer. In fact, I should tell you right up front, I am going to sound like these wonderful professionals, but I am not one of them. I'm going to write the crazy crap that has worked for me. This totally might work for you or it could totally not. I'm just giving some personal ideas and advice from my life.

If you are under the care of a physician or dietitian, please continue to be under their care and do exactly what they have asked of you.

Dieting can make us feel miserable. Dieting can actually feel depressing and a constant reminder to us about the things we don't like about our bodies. It is time to start loving ourselves and love life again!

First, I want you to name three things you love about your body. I'll tell you mine first. I love my curves! I really do! I love them all! I have the best curvy hips, curvy thighs, curvy butt. I love them!

I also love my eyes. My eyes are big, blue and beautiful! They attract for miles! I love them!

And, it's a tie between my smile, my hands and my freckles. I love these things about my body. They make me feel happy and I love that they are uniquely mine. Your turn!

The reason I want you to write it down, is because sometimes we get so focused on dieting, we forget to love of our bodies and the unique features only we have.

Name three things you love about your body and why you love them!

I want you to promise me, if dieting has become your constant lifestyle, that you will only limit the dieting to 30-60 days. Promise!

Within this time frame, I want you to learn how to make better, lifestyle decisions. A diet should only be used as a kick-start, not a constant way of living.

Food choices, the time you eat, how often you are eating and your body's motion routine are all habits you should be changing, adding or deleting all together in order to lose weight.

I wanted to lose ten pounds. I had been busy, stressed out, not taking care of my body and putting my needs last on the list. I turned around and really noticed my weight was getting out of control if I kept going down the same path. I made some changes and little adjustments.

Here is how I lost ten pounds, stopped over-spending, over-eating and how I continue to maintain my weight while enjoying a healthy lifestyle.

I set my goals in scripts.

SCRIPT: I will lose ten pounds.

SCRIPT: I will eat less sugar.

SCRIPT: I will not eat like my children. My body is different from theirs.

SCRIPT: I will increase my budget for healthy foods and decrease my spending on the bad stuff.

DAILY DO: I stopped eating and drinking so much sugar. Shut down the sugar show. I make better food choices.

Sugar is toxic. Google that stuff. It's nasty. Especially white sugars.

BUT SUGAR TASTES AMAZING!!! UGH!!! I know! I totally get it! I am addicted! I love sugar! I am not proposing we run into the streets, picket and riot, shutting down every cake and cupcake factory in America! But, I am suggesting that your home and life does not operate like a sugar factory.

Sugar does taste wonderful. Sugar makes everything wonderful! But, we just need to enjoy it in a healthy way. I noticed I was adding lots of creamer in my coffee, drinking more wine at night, eating more breads, enjoying a cupcake daily, and drinking sodas all day long. Add it all up and that's a lot of sugars. So, I cut it down a lot. A lot.

Instead of three cups of coffee with creamer full of delicious sugar, I keep it down to one big cup in the morning. And I love that cup!

I love wine at night, especially after a crazy busy day or celebrating success! But, I don't drink every night. And when I do, it's just a glass or two. Not a whole bottle. I savor each sip and really enjoy wine with my husband, and great food, talking about life and enjoying one another.

I rarely have breads. I enjoy breads served at restaurants and special events. But, I choose to not eat breads every day. Staying away from bread helps me feel good. I feel like have more energy when I don't weigh myself down with gluten and gut filling breads. Get creative on how to get rid of bread in your life.

I don't have a cupcake every day, but I do enjoy treats when called for. A friend's party, celebrations, an amazing night out. I do enjoy sugar! I just save it for the special days, not the every day. And I love to bake! So, if I know I will be baking one day, I don't have a bunch of sugar the previous days. It's a good balance.

Sodas. I love a good bubbly of soda. My favorite is Coke. I'm a huge Coke fan. Fill a frosty mug with ice and Coca-Cola. Add a straw. I could drink that amazing concoction every day! But it is massive amounts of sugar.

Go look right now and see how much sugar is in a can of soda or a bottle. WOW!

Now, I still enjoy my sodas. But, instead of drinking the big bottle sizes all day long, I enjoy a Coke or soda a few times a week, smaller sizes, and not daily. I love them even more when I do! Such a sweet treat!

Dieting can be very expensive. When we purchase fat-free, sugar-free, calorie-free, gluten-free, and fresh, that all adds up too! Eating healthy can be expensive. So, how do we continue a lifestyle of health while not breaking the bank and having to spend our 401k on healthy foods?

I increased our budget for groceries and fresh food. You can't keep your grocery budget the same and think you are going to lose weight and maintain a healthy weight. We changed our eating lifestyle which meant we moved more money into the eating healthy budget. We buy more fresh groceries instead of fast-food junk.

Pastas, breads, hot dogs, cheese, and all those delicious calories make for easy, less-expensive dinners, but they also make for more calories in our butts.

Make small adjustments. Our dinners are full of lean meats, fish, fresh and frozen vegetables, and lots of color! If your dinners and meals are tan, white, cream and have no bright colors, it is time for healthy adjustments.

Other ways I lost weight and changed my lifestyle was not eating late, not putting food in my body until I am hungry, not constantly snacking and being sure to move by body every day. If you make these small adjustments in small doses every day, they become big healthy habits that you learn to live every day.

I do not eat big meals all day. My body cannot process that in my forties. I only eat when I am hungry. I listen to my body hunger. I know when I need food and I eat wonderful, light meals.

I do not snack all day long. Do you even realize what you are putting in your body every few minutes, every few hours, every day? It's a great way to save money! If you aren't snacking all day, you aren't spending all day.

Get active. Your body needs to move. If you are trying to lose weight or live healthy, you've got to move. I am not talking about joining the hottest gym, hottest hot yoga class or getting the hottest personal trainer, they are cute! I'm just telling you to move. Take a walk. Take a bike ride. Start moving and you will start losing. Change up some little habits of sitting in front of a computer and t.v. and start moving into big changes. Motion matters.

Another way I maintain my weight is I don't eat like my kids. I am forty-five years old. My metabolism and hormones are completely different from that of a four or five year old. My ten year old male twins all the way up to my twenty-one year old son do not have my body.

All five of my boys are growing crazy! Always growing out of jeans, out of socks, out of my mind! I am not growing crazy. Just growing crazy about the constant clothes and shoes we need around here! So, I can't eat like them. And I don't. My body can no longer handle what children eat. I am a beautiful, grown adult. That one change alone changed a lot for me and my body.

I eat for me. Often, we can find something to eat together, but if it is a hot dog, chicken nugget or heavy pasta night, count me out. I can make a salad or sandwich that works for my body. I can usually find a left-over in the fridge that is healthy for me and my body can process it overnight, not in fourteen days.

I plan our meals and lunch ideas on Sunday's. I try and make sure they are healthy. Sometimes, the boys and men in this house need more calories than me. So, I usually have an idea for my stomach while trying to fill the bottomless pits called "stomachs of growing boys". My family is great. They usually eat my home-cooked meals and enjoy most of my cooking. But, we don't always eat the same things. That is how I maintain my weight and lose weight. Don't eat like your kids.

Cooking at home. It's another small adjustment to the lifestyle that will save you calories and lots of money! We will talk more about this whole cooking idea in Tool #18.

If I diet, it is only for a few weeks. I never diet for long periods of time. My diets usually occur a little before and after vacations, holidays and the winter season. My healthy eating lifestyle occurs the rest of the time so I don't have to diet for long periods or all the time. I can also enjoy sugar too and enjoy the moment!

I stopped dieting, and started living and loving life!

MONEY MANTRA: Increase my grocery budget to eat healthy. Decrease my sugar spending.

TOOL #11

STAY AWAY

How do I control my spending and stay focused on my budget and savings? I stay away from places that I tend to spend a lot of money within. Let me explain.

Here in Colorado, we have some of the most beautiful, outdoor malls throughout our state. They are wonderful for shopping, hanging out by the fire pits along the walk ways, great eateries and many of my favorite stores are lined up in a row just for me and our family. I have the availability and opportunity to swing by a mall in all directions that I live. From the mountains to the eastern plains, and deep in the city, the malls are everywhere. But I choose to stay away.

I haven't been inside a mall for years and the outdoor malls, I was either working there or looking for something specific. Ran in, got it, and left.

Are malls bad? No! They are wonderful places of employment and shopping, meeting many of our needs for clothing and home goods. But, if you are like me and tend to over-spend in a mall, you need to stay away.

If you are working in a retail setting at a store, but you spend all your money at the mall, that's not working. Let's try something else. You might need to find another job where you don't spend money every day. If you are really serious about stopping your over-spending, you can't work at a place that you spend your paycheck.

I worked retail for many years. They were great jobs when I was young and grey jobs to work along the way to help pay bills for my family. During those years, I only brought home part of my paychecks because I loved the employee discounts and clearance racks! So, unless I own the retail store, I don't work retail. It curbs my over-spending.

What are other places that you can stay away from to stop over-spending?

Fast-Food drive-thru's, Restaurants, Bars, Casino's, Warehouse & Big Box Stores to name a few places that you walk in planning on spending about $100 and you walk out with a $500 bill. Whaaaa???

Just stay away.

What places are your weaknesses that you should stay away from? List 10.

Beyond places, there are also things and people that you should stay away from. For instance, if you keep hanging out with a particular girlfriend who wants to hang out at the mall, then go to the bar, then do it again the next day, choosing to stay away from that person a bit will save you a lot of money. Or, just try to hang out without spending so much money all the time. Get creative in your friendship. Try not to spend money together, that's a big over-spending problem.

Things like the phone, the computer, gadgets and the T.V., should also be time restricted. The constant ads, the constant sales, the constant ability to spend by pushing click, click and click. Things need to be controlled and you need to control them, especially the things that tend to control your kids. If they control you, imagine the control they have on your children. Take back your control.

What are the top three things and people making you over-spend?

How could you take control over those things and control the relationships with those people to help you not spend so much money?

Learn to stop over-spending by stop over-screening. Screen time from phone, computer gadgets and T.V. can over-spend us into oblivion! Screen time and the constant information thrown at us can cause our hearts to be discontented and anxiety to creep in. Don't allow these things to enter your home or your heart.

DAILY DO: Set goals for shopping screen time. Also set specific goals of what to stay away from each day.

If you say it out loud, it will be. I am very verbal about the screen time in our home. Last night, I warned the boys they had ten more minutes on their screens and then it was dinner time and relaxing or reading time the rest of the evening. It was a great night together! Actually looking into their eyes, having conversations, people time.

I specifically set the goal yesterday to not go to the mall or any stores. I didn't HAVE to run anywhere or spend money. I did make one purchase online and only what I needed. It was great! So satisfying to not over-spend!

Today, I do need to pick-up a picture I had professionally framed. It is in a wonderful store that I love to shop! But, it's not in my budget to shop it today. I am only walking in for the picture pick-up. It's my goal! I'm going to meet it!

I don't want to spend money at fast-food tonight or restaurants, so I have already planned a meal and it is in the crock-pot! Boom! Another goal met! No over-spending tonight!

Goals set, goals met! Goals are how you stop over-spending. Make your list, say it out loud, scratch off when completed. It feels amazing!

SCRIPT: "I don't need to go there today. What else could I do to get that I item?"

SCRIPT: "I need to write my goals and my budget today so I stay away from that place."

SCRIPT: "If I go in there, I spend too much money. I don't want to do that anymore."

SCRIPT: "I can't control myself in that store. Where else can I find those items for less?"

SCRIPT: "Cash is king. I'm leaving the debit card at home and only paying cash."

Here's another tip of how I live my life debt-free and don't over-spend. If I absolutely must go into a mall or retail big box store, or that wonderful warehouse full of delightful goodies, I leave my debit card at home. I bring cash. I spend cash only.

If you haven't cut up your cards already, do it now. And never bring a credit card with you shopping. Ever. And never open a store credit card. Ever.

Learn how to shop with cash and leave the debit card home, often. Watch how much money you save each month using this tool.

Also, when you don't spend so much, you don't have so much. Watch how the stuff coming in slows down. That feels amazing too in your space!

MONEY MANTRA: I am going to stay away from this place, this thing, this person, because they make me over-spend. I will be in control of my spending if I stay away.

TOOL #12

STOP PLAYING STUPID, START LIVING SMART

STUPID GIRL, ALL YOU HAD YOU WASTED.
-GARBAGE

I may have just called you stupid. I get to because I'm writing the book and you're reading it and because I have been stupid!

If there is a level of stupid, I managed to do all levels. If there was a stupid way of doing things, I completely did it that way. If there was a stupid decision to be made, I made them all.

But, I know your secret. See, you are like me. You are actually very bright, very smart. You just continue to act and play stupid because then you have no responsibility in the stupid decisions and consequences, right?

If you play stupid housewife who doesn't know anything about the bank accounts, the budget, the bills, insurances, nothing, then you get to keep playing stupid and helpless. Right?

If you play stupid business owner who doesn't know where the money is coming and going, then you can just keep spending and not look at those books. Right?

If you play stupid, then you act stupid and do really stupid things. I know. I did. All of it!

I played stupid from money and finances and didn't want to take the responsibility or be responsible for my spending. Insert stupid decision and serious consequences right here.

Then, in my businesses, I just wanted to spend and grow and move forward. Budget? What budget? The money is flowing, just spend! Insert really stupid decision and serious consequences here, again.

By playing and acting stupid, I have had to live the consequences of those decisions, I have lost it all. I have wasted it all.

The worst part about playing stupid and suffering consequences of those stupid decisions is how my family had to suffer. Playing stupid causes suffering.

I have broken us financially, I have broken my marriage, I broke my business, I broke me. Broke and broken. All because I wanted to play dumb and ignorant and unaware.

So, I started living and acting smart. Really smart. In finances, budgeting, money, financial planning, and anything I could train my mind about money and finances, I did just that.

I attend conferences, listen to podcasts, and I am reading every day from authors who can teach me about money. I continue to learn and fill my mind with insights on all topics about money and budgeting and being successful in business.

DAILY DO: Read a book, listen to podcast, watch video, learn something new about finances. Never stop learning and listening to experts.

Be sure to learn from successful people! If you are listening to friends and family who are not successful, you will not be either. Someone who has made it, done it, lives it! Those are the "experts". Learn from them.

WAIT! That makes me an EXPERT! I have made it, done it and continue to live it! But, I made all the wrong decisions in playing stupid for so long with my money management.

I want you to stop playing stupid. You know more than you think you know. You can do more than you think you can do. And you can be more successful than you can possibly imagine!

When you don't know about the budget:

SCRIPT: "I want to know my budget and what I need to be spending. Can you help me know that information?"

When you need to learn everything:

SCRIPT: "I don't have access to our accounts. I don't know how to pay the bills. I need to learn all of that. Can you show me how?"

When someone else runs your business books:

SCRIPT: "I appreciate all you have done for my business, but I need you to explain every penny to me and what the budget is for each account. I need to know everything. Can you show me the books?"

When someone is enabling your over-spending bad habits:

SCRIPT: "I want you to stop enabling me to make really bad decisions with my money. I need your help to stop. Will you help me with my budget and help me stick to a budget?"

What are three ways you could get smart about your finances today?

I live smart in my money every day. First, I always know what is in our accounts. Everything. I know our banking accounts, retirement accounts, savings accounts, business accounts. All of it.

I also know our budget for each account and I know our goals for those accounts. I know what I can and cannot spend from those accounts. I know the bills coming and going from those accounts. I am informed constantly about the accounts. About all the money.

Every day I listen to an expert. Whether it is listening to the Dave Ramsey Radio Show, Christy Wright Podcast, or Rachel Cruze You Tube Videos, I am watching and learning from experts. I am filling my brain and heart constantly with the good stuff! I process a lot of the information and put it into action in my personal and professional life.

You have access to some of the most amazing experts in money management, financial planning and access to wonderful ideas about how to stop over-spending and master your money. Make it a habit! Daily Do!

Daily, I am in a book. I love authors that are experts in their field. I read a book about business every month. I read a book about bettering myself every month. So, I have at least two books I am reading every month.

I have a Personal Reading List in my office which lists books I want to personally grow and become a better person from reading. I also have a Professional Reading List that lists great books to help me be a successful business owner and leader. I check them off as I read each month. I learn and grow from all of them!

This is how I stop playing stupid and start living smart.

MONEY MANTRA: Stop playing stupid. I am really smart about money and finances.

TOOL #13

SOMETHING IN, SOMETHING OUT

Lucky Tool #13! This is one of my favorites! It's a tool I use all the time! It's actually not a tool or tip, it's become a RULE in our house! As an organizing professional and fanatic, I am so excited for you to learn this tool!

DAILY DO: Whenever we bring a new item into the house, whether that is a piece of clothing, new toy, furniture, papers, magazines, mail, sports equipment, shoes, anything that we will now keep or be using in our home, something has to leave. Something has to go!

Something must go out, either to the trash, recycling, garage sale storage, give to friend or family, sell it online or sell at consignment. It's out!

Something in, something out. When you learn to live by this simple tool and rule, your home and space become peaceful, organized, and filled with only the things you love and only the things you use.

Also, when you learn to get rid of things, it develops a great habit of learning to not spend so much on things.

When you think through the process and ask yourself, "If I purchase this, what am I going to get rid of?" Sometimes, it makes you stop a purchase, or realize you can still use the things you already have or sometimes you don't want to throw something out. See how it works?

Lucky #13 also helps you make money instead of over-spending money. When something comes in, something gets sold. Often, my boys grow out of clothes and shoes quickly. My growing boys can be expensive. So, recently when Jacob brought in two new pairs of shoes, we sold two used shoes on consignment. What we made from our consignment sale actually paid us back for one of the pairs of new shoes. Whoo-Hoo!

And when Jacob, Jett and Jonah all needed new pants for their constant growing legs, we had sold so many items on consignment, that we were able to get all the boys new pants at the consignment store and they were paid for from our account! It felt like getting pants for free! So helpful to our clothes budget!

I have been re-decorating my home on the main level. I am creating a blue and white oasis that is relaxing and feels comfortable every day! I painted the guest bath deep blue and I am adding a white mirror and white and blue decorations.

Because of the new items that came in, I am getting the used items out. I am selling a mirror, decorations and towel set online. Those sales will help to pay me back for the cost of paint, the new mirror and new decor.

Are you getting it? Something in, something out.

What could you throw out, recycle, give away or sell today?

Tip: I usually start in one room or space. Complete it and then move on to another.

SCRIPT: "I brought it in, what can go out?"

SCRIPT: "If I buy something new, something used has to go. Do I really need to buy this right now?"

SCRIPT: "Choose ten things, sell them online or at consignment. Then, I will shop with the money I make from those sales for the new stuff."

Something in, something out helps you to stop your over-spending when you think it through. When you are constantly throwing stuff away or watching stuff go out, it really makes you think about the money that you are spending, the money you might be wasting and the money you could be making!

Something in, something out gives you great insight into your constant spending habits and excessive stuff habits.

Start living this simple lifestyle tool today!

MONEY MANTRA: Every single thing has a cost. If I buy this right now, I need to sell something else.

TOOL #14

STOP WASTING,
START CONSERVING

DON'T WASTE YOUR LIFE
WISHING, HOPING, WAITING FOR A BETTER DAY
YOU KNOW THAT WOULD BE A SHAME
SHINE, SHINE YOUR LIFE
BIGGER, BRIGHTER FOR THE WHOLE WORLD TO SEE
PLAY YOUR PART IN HISTORY
DON'T WASTE YOUR LIFE.

-GINNY OWENS

We waste food, we waste time, we waste energy, we waste paper, we waste toothpaste, we waste! We all do it!

When we waste, we are throwing out money too. You may think you're just wasting old food, or leaving on those lights isn't that big of a deal, or filling your schedule with activities that do no matter is just "busyness" or that stack of papers to recycle feels better than throwing in the trash. We are wasting! We are wasting money in all these decisions!

Throwing out food is throwing out money. Groceries and food are one of the biggest, expensive items in our budget and we waste so much money on food. Instead of wasting, start conserving. The way I watch our food budget and wastefulness in the kitchen is knowing what is in my pantry, knowing what I need in the fridge.

I make a list to shop, purchasing the ingredients that make lunches, dinners and purchase snacks that don't expire quickly. When I purchase fruit and veggies, it's usually just for a couple days worth. Buying fresh is expensive, just purchase what you need for a few days. Go back to the store to buy fresh when needed. It saves so much money each week and you waste less!

I just returned from the local grocery store here in town. I spent $65.00 to feed us for the next five days before vacation. Spring Break is next week and I don't want to leave a lot in the fridge to spoil while we travel.

Before heading to the store, I made a mental note of what I already have, what I can work with and what I need.

At the store, I took my time, bought frozen and fresh, only what we need, won't quickly expire and bought local. I found a family size Salmon on sale for $5.00, so I bought 3 of those beauties! That will feed us three to five meals! Then, I bought four cereals and got the milk for free with a store coupon. The boys will eat that cereal in two days, and that milk will be gone in three days. No wasting here!

I don't want to waste veggies and fresh items, so I just purchased a head of lettuce, carrots and a cucumber. That can make salads for lunches and dinners the next few days and it will be gone.

HEALTHY TIP* I don't eat breads often, so I substitute bread with a big leaf of lettuce and wrap ingredients in the lettuce and not bread. It's also cheaper to use lettuce then breads. You are welcome!

Everything I purchased was on sale. I found a loaf of bread for the boys reduced to .25 cents! I found a cough medicine marked down to $2.29. Bought two! My Cottage Cheese was on sale for $1.29. Do you see what I'm doing? Looking for the best deals, looking for the lowest cost, looking to not waste food or money.

Eat left-overs. We eat a lot of leftovers in the Chase Cave! I love to make a left-over chili on Sundays. Just throw it all in! The boys scarf if down. Money Saver! Less Waste!

You can put any left-overs in a crock-pot and cook it all day. Let it simmer and smells delicious in the house. It also feels like a new meal and not from the night before. Mix it up!

How can I make five adjustments to my shopping habits and eating habits to not waste food?

I hate to waste my time. It is precious to me. I hate missing out. I don't have a lot of time. I hate getting it wrong. I hate it! My time is so important to me and my family. How I spend it matters.

I am very controlling of my time and I am a constant guardian it. Are you? Or are you constantly wasting your time? Giving it to others too much? Not blocking out time for yourself? So busy you miss things? So busy you forget things? So busy, you are always running around, not on time? I get it. I've done that.

I learned to respect the saying, "Time is Money." Do you believe that? Do you believe that your time equals money? I believe it!

SCRIPT: "Time is Money."

When I waste my office and writing time, I lose money. When I lose time not scheduling clients, that is a loss of revenue. When I am so busy, I forget to make it to an appointment, money is gone. When I just decide to be lazy and not accomplish tasks that need to be completed that day, I could lose contracts worth thousands. Time = Money.

DAILY DO: If you get organized, you will reduce your waste of time substantially. The night before a big meeting or trip or place to be, I get everything in order and everything organized. Even my keys have a place, so when I leave early in the morning, those keys are right there. Ready to go! That includes the kids! They need to have their jackets, backpacks and shoes in their spot, ready to go! Save time by being organized!

How do I waste my time every day?

What actions can I put into place to stop wasting that time every day?

In a house that has raised five boys and two dogs, we can waste some serious energy! Leave lights on for days, turn up and burn up gas and heat for months, and that does not include all the electrical outlets with computers and gadgets in them!

This home is flowing with energy! Energy costs can be extremely expensive. Energy can burst the budget! We need to learn to conserve.

SCRIPT: "Turn it off!"

I shared with the boys about the cost each month of our energy needs. I explained that the higher the energy bill each month, the less fun stuff we would be doing, the less eating out we would be enjoying, the less cool clothes we would be buying and the less toys they would be getting. That struck a nerve!

It became a contest as to who could turn a light out first? How low could we go with the thermostat without experiencing freezer burn? Could we beat our lowest cost that month?

Jonah follows us around and turns off a light every time we leave a room. "Jonah, I am coming back to this room." "Mom, you are not in the room right now! Save energy, save money!"

My work here is done.

What are five new habits we could start to save energy and save money in our home?

Goal: Lower energy costs by $25, $50, $75 or $100 per month. (Circle One)

Do you have a paper fetish? What I mean by that is, do you bring papers into your home and they never leave?

Newspapers, paper bills, paper advertisements, notebook paper, legal paper, printing paper, paper invitations, paper books, paper recipes, paper receipts. And on and on the paper goes.

It piles up. Then that pile becomes another pile. Those piles get moved into another room with other piles of papers. And after a few years, your home has become a really expensive paper storage unit.

Do you know that piles of paper steal your energy and your peace? Do you know that piles of paper suck your joy? Do you know that you do not ever need that amount of paper?

Do you have a drawer full of paper warranties for all your vacuums, appliances, and expensive purchases? I giggle a little bit inside at you. Sorry! There is absolutely no reason to hold on to or file or keep a paper warranty. First of all, we live in the 2000's. Everything is computerized and online these days. Everything! If you are concerned about needing that paper warranty for some crazy reason (still giggling a little bit at you :) then learn how to take a copy of it by scanning it into a computer. Place it in a computer file titled "warranties". Then put that paper warranty into a shredding machine or a recycle bin or have a burning party and make smores. Get rid of the paper!

We need very little paper in our lives and we certainly do not need piles of papers in our homes, rooms, offices and living spaces. Papers served a purpose and now are waste.

What are three piles of paper that I will take care of today? Goal: file, scan to computer, recycle, or just throw it out.

We can waste just about anything, right? Think about all the little things we waste every single day?

Toothpaste, make-up, hairspray, nail polish, cleaning products, paper towels, shampoo and conditioners, coffee creamer, unfinished drinks, running water, gasoline in our cars and on and on the wasting goes. But, we don't have to waste all the time. We can get better at not being wasteful for every single thing.

One of the best ways to not waste is to CONSERVE.

I looked up the definition of "Conserve" on my computer dictionary, which utilizes the New Oxford American Dictionary.

1. Protect from harm or destruction.

2. Prevent the wasteful or harmful overuse of a resource.

3. Preserve.

Doesn't conserving sound wonderful? Don't you think maybe we all could protect, prevent, preserve food, protect our time, prevent the waste of energy, prevent the constant waste of paper, and any little thing daily? Me too!

It's a heart thing. It's a maturity thing. It's being a better person thing.

Choose to not waste. Choose to conserve. You can tell what kind of person you are, you can tell where your heart is, you can tell if you have moved into maturity, by how much you waste and conserve.

I had to get better. I know you can be better.

I had to stop over-spending by wasting. I know you can stop being wasteful too.

What actions and new habits can I take to conserve every single thing I spend money on in my life?

Food, gas, cars, clothes, toiletries, papers, school, alcohol, energy, utility bills. Every. Single. Thing.

MONEY MANTRA: I am not going to waste money. I will conserve any way possible. I will stop throwing away my hard-earned money.

TOOL #15

TWENTY-MINUTE-TIDY

CLEAN UP, CLEAN UP
EVERYBODY EVERYWHERE
CLEAN UP, CLEAN UP
EVERYBODY DO THEIR SHARE.
                    -BARNEY

I know, I know! There is a ten-minute-tidy up. But, I can't do it in ten minutes. In our house, to clean up, pick up, and tidy up, we need at least twenty minutes. Therefore, the twenty-minute-tidy.

DAILY DO: Twenty-minute-tidy in my home, office and budget.

Before school this morning, I had the twins, Jettson and Jonah, do a twenty-minute-tidy with me. We got so much completed!

Emptied the dishwasher, loaded the dishwasher and it is currently running a load. Cleaned the glass doors to the backyard because the dogs like to leave their muddy paw-prints on them. Vacuumed the main level carpet areas. Cleaned the kitchen counter tops. Went around the whole house and gathered trash for trash day pick-up this morning. It's all out at the curb, ready to go! Picked up toys and put them in their toy bins. Threw away papers hanging out on the kitchen counter and filed the ones they wanted to keep. The boys started laundry upstairs for their dirty clothes, I started a load of laundry downstairs for Dan and I. This is all in twenty minutes folks! You can get so much completed.

Afterwards, the twins brushed their teeth, grabbed their backpacks and walked to the bus. I got dressed and I am on my way to serve a client in a couple hours, helping her get organized.

After work, I will come home to a clean house, all because we took twenty minutes to tidy up this morning.

When we take the time to clean up a little each day, we won't get stuck cleaning all day or many days.

Learn how to master the twenty-minute-tidy and make sure to get your roommate or family involved! Everyone who lives together pitches in and does their share! They help make the mess, they help clean up the mess.

What could you get done today in a twenty-minute-tidy?

"What does the twenty-minute-tidy have to do with helping me stop over-spending?" Great question! Glad you asked! It means you are ready to master your money!

When you are organized and you tidy-up your home, office and finances daily, you tend to not over-spend because you know what you have, you know what you need, you know what you can sell, you know what you don't use.

You find that you become tired of picking up the same things, buying double of everything or wasting your money on things you don't even use. And you know that because you do a twenty-minute-tidy all the time. You become master of your domain and master of your money. All due to a little tidying up.

Yes! You can do a twenty-minute-tidy or less on your finances every day. In the morning, I look at the bank balances. I also look at our budgets. Where are we at? How are we doing? Is everything being paid properly? How much is my budget today? I don't want to overspend, so I do a twenty-minute-tidy with my money every day. Sometimes, it's a five-minute-tidy on money, but get in the habit of knowing your money.

I do that in the morning and often, I do it at night before closing down my office or computer for the evening. Just a quick tidy up on money makes you feel aware, in control and on top of it!

A twenty-minute-tidy on my money gives me peace to relax at night and sleep sound knowing the bills are paid, profits were made, it's a great sleeping aid!

I have a couple hours before my organizing client today, so I am finishing this tool chapter for you and I can complete other quick and simple tasks in that time.

I will complete the loads of laundry we put in this morning, I am about to put pork in the crockpot for dinner tonight and I want to organize my office desk this morning. The papers have been creeping in! All of that combined will take about twenty minutes. I'm about to do a twenty-minute-tidy, just not all at the same time. See how that works?

CONFIDENCE. When we continually tidy up our space, we produce confidence in ourselves to make good decisions, feel good within our spaces, and only live with what we love. Tidying up produces confidence and if you want to stop over-spending, a great characteristic to own is confidence. Having confidence in our money choices, over our habits, and feeling confident in finances is amazing! This is how you stop over-spending.

SCRIPT: "I am confident that I have all the power I need to make good money, be good at money and be good to others with my money."

SCRIPT: "I will learn to be more confident in my money choices and spending habits by always learning. I will rule my money in my confidence!"

Have confidence in yourself about mastering your money habits. And it starts with a twenty-minute-tidy in your home, office and budget.

MONEY MANTRA: I have confidence in mastering my money and I will become more confident by completing the twenty-minute-tidy in my home, office and budget every day.

TOOL #16

STOP BEING SELFISH, START YOUR SELF-CARE

BE GOOD TO YOURSELF WHEN NOBODY ELSE
WILL, BE GOOD TO YOURSELF
YOU'RE WALKING A HIGH WIRE, YOU'RE IN
A CROSS FIRE, BE GOOD TO YOURSELF.
                                   -JOURNEY

Many of us, especially women, have a horrible way of caring for ourselves. Often, we start self-care only AFTER finding out we are over-weight, over-stressed, and have cancer.

How ridiculous? How backwards? And how selfish of us that we did not care for ourselves and now our loved ones have to care for us?

Stop being a martyr. That syndrome went out years ago. Start your self-care and get over the lies that caring for yourself is "selfish". That is just false!

I put on my schedule and put into the budget "spa time," "alone time," and "healthy living time." I do this for my personal health and so I can live longer for my family. My family needs me! I need to be the Mom to my sons, and my husband needs me to be his Wife. Therefore, I self-care.

I care for myself and my body regularly. From hair, nails, massage, and sauna time. From eating out alone, reading a good book, listening to great messages that are inspiring and motivating often. From eating healthy, cooking healthy, learning something new to grow my mind and moving my body regularly, it's all on my schedule, it's all in my budget, it's all how I live my life and it's all good!

I do not feel guilty when I am getting a massage or spending a little more on healthy organic food at the grocery store. I do not feel guilty of going for a walk instead of cleaning the dishes. I do not feel guilty about attending a conference to learn from experts and move my mind. I do not feel guilty about working hard so I can self-care and care for my family. I don't! And you shouldn't either.

SCRIPT: "Self-care is not selfish. Not caring for myself is not healthy."

What are three ways you can take care of yourself physically, emotionally, mentally that cost money?

Now, go put those three things you listed onto your schedule and place them into a category in your budget.

I have an envelope that I place cash into every month just for this! I wrote on the front of the envelope "Personal Care & Spa". I fill it with $200 dollars each month. From that budget, I can do so much! Get my hair done, get a massage, and eat out at my favorite sushi spot, by myself! It's so wonderful and self-healing.

There are other self-care actions that I take that don't cost anything. I read many books, I listen to free radio and podcasts, I exercise right here in my home, I can get outside and ride a bike or take a long walk. I can go to the library or bookstore and relax, getting lost in a fabulous mystery. I can clean my entire house that gets my body moving and is good exercise for muscles I don't use anymore! I can hang out with a friend or good neighbor and catch up for free!

What are three ways you can self-care that do not cost any money?

Why do we have a fear of taking care of ourselves? Is it because someone called you selfish? Is it the world around us telling us we are selfish? Is it our church? Our friends? Our parents? They know how to guilt trip!

There are many mixed messages about self-care out there. But, the real truth is, we need to take care of ourselves today so we can have a better future tomorrow.

I just had to take care of two teeth in my mouth at the Dentist. They both had to be filled and crowned. It sucked! But, it felt great taking care of them now, so I won't lose those teeth quickly and I will have a better future with them. Because of my self-care, my teeth look and feel great!

I wanted to lose some weight this year. Nothing crazy, just about ten pounds. So, did I just continue to eat sugar, eat breads, eat like my kids, not get active and not take care of myself? Nope. I had to take action and self-care. Taking good care of my body and health is not selfish.

Self-care includes SLEEP! Last night, I took a sleeping aid and slept from 9:00pm to 8:15am. YAAASSSS! I feel like a new woman! I can conquer the world! Sleep is so vital to our health and great self-care!

It was not selfish of me to get a good nights sleep. It would have been selfish of me not to.

Now, some of you ARE being selfish. You only care for yourself. You only spend money on yourself. You only think of yourself. You only do things for yourself. Yes, some people are selfish. And if that is you, then knock it off!

You can tell if you are being selfish if you over-spend money. Over-spending is over-selfing. You are only thinking of yourself in that moment and not the consequences that you or others will have to face due to your over-spending. You are not respecting your work or your spouses work to earn that money, so you disrespect by over-spending. How selfish?

DAILY DO: Stop being selfish. Start spending my money with respect.

When you respect your money, and respect the one who earned it, including yourself, you will learn to not over-spend it.

We are being selfish when we know we should not spend a certain amount, but do anyway. We are being selfish when we continue to just spend for ourselves and not bless others. We are being selfish when we are just thinking of ourselves in the moment of spending.

Change your habit of being selfish and you will stop over-spending.

SCRIPT: "Am I being selfish about this purchase right now? Why am I spending this money?"

SCRIPT: "If I spend this money today, will it hurt anyone or will it bless someone?"

There is nothing wrong with spending money. We need to spend money to survive! It's the over-spending that is wrong. It's the thinking we need all this crap to survive that is wrong.

Once I realized that I was being selfish when I was over-spending daily, I grew up in my money management. I got really good with my money! I developed better spending habits that were not self-absorbed, self-emotional, or self-promoting. My spending became family oriented, meeting others needs first and then self-care for my well-being became a part of that as well. It's a great balance and makes for a great life!

MONEY MANTRA: Self-Care needs to be a part of my lifestyle and a part of my budget. It's important to me and my family that I take good care of myself.

TOOL #17

CONTROL THE HEAD-JUNK

OH, WE'RE NEVER GONNA SURVIVE UNLESS WE GET A
LITTLE CRAZY
OTHER PEOPLE WALKING ROUND THROUGH MY HEAD...
                                        -SEAL

Can you believe that we all have head-junk? I'm not really sure that's an actual word or classification, but it perfectly describes my brain activity! And let me tell you, I have got some serious head-junk people!

From Mommy and Daddy issues, to fears and anxiety, to how I dissect conversations, to how I feel about myself or lots of head-junk! It is real people!

But, you know what I have learned over my forty-something years? The head-junk can be controlled, cleaned out, dealt with. I can change it. And it's really just that, JUNK!

Looking up the definition of "junk" was perfect! This totally sums it up:

1. old or discarded articles that are considered useless or of little value.

2. worthless writing, talk or ideas.

YEP! That is my head-junk! Useless or of little value to my life! Worthless ideas for my heart and my soul! It is all junk! And I want to control it. Don't you?

So, how do I control my head-junk? First, I am honest about it. I need to understand what it is specifically. My thought process, how I am feeling, listen to my heart and my soul for the truth.

I have some serious Mommy and Daddy issues. My childhood really screwed me up all the way into adulthood. This fact can affect my thought process. These issues can affect my money spending habits. So, before action, I process.

I think them through. I process my thoughts and feeling first. I process to clear my head. I process to know truth and state the truth. Then, I can take action in my life and in my spending.

SCRIPT: "My parents told me I am a bad person and a bad parent. That is not the truth. The truth is, I am a good person. I am doing my best parenting and living my best life!"

DAILY DO: State the truth and control the head-junk.

My childhood does not determine my adulthood. I do. The things that have been said to me, do not determine my truth, my life or who I am. I do. My crazy parents do not mean I have to be crazy too. I decide my crazy!

I also deal with some fears and anxiety in my head. Some of them rational, some are irrational. My fears include the fear of losing one of my children or my husband. They include the fear of failing. Other fears I have include the fear of not meeting goals or not being successful. Fears of growing old.

I have anxiety about speaking in front of huge crowds, I have anxiety about leaving the house sometimes. I have anxiety about being in certain situations or having to talk to certain people. UGH! The head-junk can be over-whelming! I can get wrapped up in my fears and my anxieties in my head!

So, I process. Process the thought and the feeling. What is the truth? Then state it.

SCRIPT: "I am feeling anxiety and I am afraid of this. But the truth is, I can handle this and I have the power to overcome my fears and anxiety about this."

DAILY DO: State the truth, control the head-junk.

I have some head-junk about dissecting conversations. I can re-live a conversation over and over analyzing what I should have said and what was actually said for hours.

What a waste of my time!

Over-analyzing conversations can be useless, of little value and worthless if not controlled. A little analysis is healthy. It keeps us from saying the wrong things at the wrong time and it helps us get better at communicating. But the over-analyzing is irrational. That needs to be controlled. So, process, then take action.

SCRIPT: "Stop over-playing and over-analyzing this conversation. It is over and done. What can I learn from it and then I need to move on".

DAILY DO: State the truth, control the head-junk.

The truth is, I am a master communicator! I love talking with others, I love having conversations with different people and I don't need to analyze them. I love writing conversations to people, I love writing in conversation in my books to an audience that wants to listen and I refuse to analyze anything that will be of no value to my life.

Analyze it to learn from it and then move on.

I have fears and anxiety about how I feel about myself. Do I look okay? I'm always wearing the wrong thing. Do I sound like an idiot? I have a tendency to say the wrong thing. Do I look fat in this? Do I have the right makeup? Am I having a good hair day? Why didn't she smile back at me?

And on and on in my head it goes! The head-junk of how I feel about myself. It can be debilitating. It can make me roll up in ball and stay in bed. Have you ever felt that way?

So, I process. And then I take action!

SCRIPT: "Why am I feeling this way about myself today? I need to control my head-junk and focus on the truth!"

I get out bed and press on through my fears and how I feel in that moment. I take control of my thoughts, and take action!

DAILY DO: State the truth and control the head-junk.

The truth is, I am bold, beautiful and my best! I have the power to overcome my fears and overcome my head-junk! I will state the truth and no longer live my life based on fears and lies. I am down-right fabulous and this world needs to watch out!

What are the out-of-control fears and anxiety I have that are making me out-of-control with my spending?

Am I over-analyzing people and conversations?

How do I feel about myself and is that really the truth?

What are three habits I can learn to control my head-junk and my spending?

The head-junk actually does control your spending. It's so interesting how our fears, anxieties, over-analyzing and our feelings about ourselves affect our spending.

If we have bad habits in our head, we have bad habits in our money. When you learn good habits in your head, you will learn to change spending behaviors in your money management. It is awesome!

When I control my head-junk, I control my spending. It feels amazing to be in control!

MONEY MANTRA: I will process and then I will take action. Controlling my thoughts, fears, and head-junk will help me control my spending.

TOOL #18

STOP EATING OUT, START EATING IN

WE THANK THE LORD FOR WHAT WE'RE ABOUT TO EAT
DINNER TIME IS A REAL GOOD TIME TO GATHER THANKFULLY
IF YOU LIKE BOTH SAVORY AND SWEET
YOU JUST CAN'T MESS WITH A PARTIAL LIST OF ALL MY
FAVORITE TREATS.
                                    -VEGGIE TALES

I touched on this in the previous tools, but I want to spend some time on this topic because it will be one of the most important tools you use in helping you stop your over-spending habits.

Eating out for breakfast, lunch, snacks and dinner is a huge budget buster!

Eating in for breakfast, lunch, snacks and dinner is a huge money savor!

I don't want you to have to eat in every single meal. It is fun eating out! It's a great time, it is great food and great adult beverages! It's wonderful eating out, but if this expense is out-of-control in your life, you must make better eating habits.

Eating Out Expenses:

How much does food and coffee cost me on average when I drive-thru or sit down at a restaurant in the morning on the way to work or school?

$_____

How much does food, plus drink and a tip cost me on average when I drive-thru or sit-down at a restaurant for lunch?

$_____

How much does food, plus drink and a tip cost me on average when I drive-thru or sit down at a restaurant for dinner?

$_____

How much am I spending on food, drinks, snacks, and tips on average every day?

$_____

How much am I spending on average per month in total eating out expenses?

$_____

Do I need to change my eating habits? _____

There are many benefits to eating at home or eating fresh. For one, it's healthier! The amount of calories, sugars, fats, and ingredients we should never put in our bodies from fast-food or restaurant food are substantial. When we shop fresh and cook at home, we eat healthy! We can control the amount of calories, sugars, fats and bad ingredients at home. We can lose weight faster, stay healthier and enjoy what we prepare knowing it is healthy for us. Our kids also learn to eat healthier now, making better choices in their adult eating habits later.

Second, eating in is good for the soul. Have you ever heard of soul food? Soul food is a variety of cuisine originating in the United States southern states. It has a history originating from Black American culture and communities within the deep South. And it is good! A traditional Soul food plate may consist of fried chicken, macaroni and cheese, collard greens and fried okra. That just made me hungry! Greasy, fried and fabulous! Thank you very much, yaaaassssss!

One of my favorite Soul food restaurants is located in Savannah, Georgia. The Lady & Sons restaurant is pure southern classics delight! From fried chicken, fried okra and fried green tomatoes. Then shrimp and grits,

Savannah crab cakes and southern gumbo. Stop it! The food is just so good! And good for the soul!

A third benefit when we cook in, eat in, and dine in, is time together. Time together is good for our souls. It is good for the souls of our children to eat with family and friends. To gather around a table and have conversations and laugh out loud together. Good food brings good love!

Make this time together. Enjoy this time together. It is precious.

SCRIPT: "Dinner time!"

Cooking, eating, and cleaning together is a simple, easy way to fall in love again, look your child in the eye again, reconnect again. Eating food at home can do that!

The dinner table in our home has become a safe place to take a deep breath and a needed break from the world. A place to relax and find love, peace and laughter. No technology allowed at the table.

A fourth and fifth benefit of cooking at home are the leftovers and less cost. You create tons of leftovers when you cook. Those leftovers are tons of meals throughout the week and the month. Easy to pack for lunch and snacks too!

I plan a leftover dinner night at least once a week. I pull out all the leftovers and place it on the counter like a buffet. The boys can pick what they want and re-heat it. Done! Dinner is served!

I also do a leftover chili often on Sunday nights, especially in the winter months. A good cup of chili is good for the soul. I just pull the leftover meats, add beans and rice, and whatever else is leftover that could work, mix it up and put them in the crockpot all day. Done! Dinner is served! And it smells great in the house too!

DAILY DO: Stop eating out so much and start eating in more.

I stopped my over-spending eating habits by eating in more. I plan my meals for the week, both lunches and dinners.

SCRIPT: "It's Sunday! Time to plan the meals!"

I make grab-n-go lunches and snacks so I can be prepared while traveling, driving, working or staying at home. I set my food budget for the month and then for each week depending on my schedule. If I'm eating out for business or with the family or girls night out, it's in the budget. I already prepared and save for that expense by not eating out every day. I sacrifice one day eating out if I know I have another night we are eating out. I eat lunch in if dinner is going to be out too!

Every meal needs to be intentionally planned and budgeted for. Make a shopping list for each meal, each ingredient. Get great ideas from websites like FoodNetwork.com and your favorite chef's. Get a Crockpot book for sure! One of the boys babysitter's, Savannah, gave me a Crockpot cooking book for Christmas many years ago. It's one of my favorite books and I use it all the time still today! Each meal has a cost and needs to be dealt with intentionally, not just throwing money at it when it happens or when you feel like eating. Get intentional about your cooking and about your eating!

I stopped my over-spending eating habits by staying at home more often too. My schedule is not so over-scheduled that I am over-spending on my eating out. Watch your schedule, watch your money.

Make a list of five lunches and five dinners you can prepare this week? Ask your family for ideas too!

On Sunday, begin the preparation and complete those five lunches and dinners as much as possible. Get all the ingredients together. Make a list and shop if needed. Date and label completed meals for fridge and freezer. Have them ready to grab-n-go throughout the week.

Frozen and fresh work great!

Remember! You are lowering your weight, lowering your stress, lowering your credit card debt when you make meals at home, eat at home and bring them with you to work too.

Let me show you how healthy eating in habits can control your over-spending habits. This is how it works for me personally. When I pack a lunch to bring to work, I am more productive at work because I work through my lunch and can leave early for the day. I don't go into a restaurant to spend money plus tip plus gas to get there and back. And then, I don't walk into the boutique next door and spend money I hadn't planned on spending on those great pair of fabulous fashion jeans and cute earrings with a shirt to match! Do I need shoes for this outfit too?

SCRIPT: "Girls, I am eating in today. I'm watching my budget and my body. Maybe next week?"

You automatically stop spending and stop over-spending when you cook from home, bring from home or stay home.

This is how you stop over-spending: You get a handle on the eating.

MONEY MANTRA: My favorite eatery is at my dinner table and it is open for business.

TOOL #19

BUDGET-BASED LIVING

```
         MONEY, MONEY, MONEY
MUST BE FUNNY IN A RICH MAN'S WORLD
         MONEY, MONEY, MONEY
ALWAYS SUNNY IN A RICH MAN'S WORLD
AHA, ALL THE THINGS I COULD DO
    IF I HAD A LITTLE MONEY
                        -ABBA
```

Budget's suck! A budget stops me from spending the way I want! A budget is too time consuming! A budget means I am living cheap and looking cheap! A Budget means I am broke! A Budget means I am having no fun!

That is what I used to think about budgeting. Do you think that way about a budget? Negatively? Angrily? Does the thought of writing and living a budget scare you?

When you hear or read the word "budget" what comes to mind?

It's a mindset thing. It's a maturity thing. It's a master-of-your-money thing. It's a BUDGET!

If you want to stop over-spending, you have to begin to set, work, follow and live by a BUDGET.

You know already how you feel about a budget. You know how you think negatively of a budget. But the truth is, a budget gives you direction. A budget gives you a roadmap. A budget gives you answers. A budget gives you a future. A budget gives you freedom! A budget is a tool to help you stop your over-spending.

Let me show me how.

Right at this very moment, I am on vacation. It is Spring Break here in Colorado . My husband and I packed up three of our boys and headed up to the mountains. We love Granby, Colorado. The ski resort is small and easy access. We rented a great town home next to the slopes. I am currently typing away, while my view is beautiful! Snow-capped mountains, snow-covered trees and huge icicles hanging from the rooftop. It's gorgeous! And it's paid for!

In December, about three months ago, I paid cash to rent our town home. Got it at a great price! We paid cash for our ski rentals, ski passes and we paid cash for our groceries and supplies yesterday for our week here. Today, I am going to spend no money. I am writing my book, drinking coffee and my creamer that I made right here in our little snow bungalow. Made a big breakfast for my men this morning, already paid for. I'm making lunch for the boys and meeting them at the slopes in a few hours, already paid for. The Salmon is defrosting in the fridge and I'll make that for dinner tonight, already paid for. We have everything we need for today. Already paid for, already staying in budget and still able to love our vacation!

My vacation is paid for in cash and I set a budget this week so we don't overspend our stay. When we drive home in a few days, we will still have money in the bank, we will not owe anything on this vacation, and we will love it even more! No use of a credit card, nothing to owe later. No bill will be coming later to pay for this vacation. It is fully funded.

My budget does not negatively affect me. My budget keeps me on track. My budget allows me the freedom to have fun and plan a great time!

Budgeting this vacation gives me freedom to take another vacation next month to California to see family and have some fun for the twins birthday and one of my boys turning 18??!?!?! We do three birthdays in one week!

Busy Birthday budget week! Plan for it! It comes around every year! Do not act surprised in your budget! Own it! Control it! Plan for important dates and vacations. Budgeting makes it all so much more peaceful, fun and less stressful!

LIE: A Budget means I am having no fun.

The TRUTH is, I have never had more fun than when I have been on a budget!

SCRIPT: Have more fun on a budget.

A budget means I am having a lot more fun, real fun, less-stressful fun, paid-for, no-debt fun! A budget gives me access to having fun now and later. I can create wonderful memories having fun on a budget!

In my money maturity, I had to grow up and out of my old way of thinking about budgeting. I used to believe the LIE that a Budget is too time consuming. The TRUTH is, there are many ways to live by and complete a budget every day, from Apps on our phones, to wonderful online tools for budgeting and like I do, just a simple Excel spreadsheet and my bank account. These tools are NOT time consuming. They are time saving.

SCRIPT: A budget saves me time and money.

No matter how you prefer writing and living by a budget, just make a decision which tools you will be using to write your budget and then living by it. Remember, your budget will save you from over-spending. Write it!

The Basics of Budgeting. When writing a budget, start with the most important items that must be the first things you pay, always:

1. Mortgage or Rent
2. Transportation, Gas & Insurance
3. Food
4. Utilities

Notice, I only put the BASICS first. You need the basics in order to survive and live. You need a home to live in. You need transportation to get you to work to make a living. You need food. Enough said there. And you need the utilities paid for in your home, such as lights, heat, cool air and water to live. You need the basics paid for in order to support you, your family and keep your children fed and warm.

I did not put a credit card bill first. I did not put any unsecured debt first. You only paid secured debt for your home and car first. Priorities! Take care of you and your family first!

Second, SAVINGS. There are two areas of savings I put into our budget, saving for an emergency and saving for an upcoming event. Let me show you what we use.

1. Emergency Fund
2. Family Fund

The Emergency Fund is based off of Dave Ramsey's book "The Total Money Makeover" and Ramsey recommends always having an Emergency account fully funded with $1,000 dollars. We do that every month! Because we need it every month! From unexpected medical bills to an unexpected water heater blowing up to lots of little and big unexpected emergencies. We have an emergency savings for the unexpected because I expect emergencies to happen, especially as the mother of five boys. Therefore, I budget.

Our Family Fund savings account includes savings for any upcoming special event, vacations and family needs. Christmas comes at the same time every year. Birthdays come at the same time every year. Vacations are set usually for the year and you know when they are coming! There are certain expenses I know are coming. I can put a date and time to them. I can also put money towards them.

We save for those upcoming events, a little bit every paycheck. It adds up! And then, we are prepared for the spending and don't need to over-spend in our ill-preparation. Save for the events you know are coming up and watch how your budget allows you freedom to enjoy those special times. Don't be stressed over it, have control over it.

Our family needs include music instruments, technology, school fees and supplies, class registration fees, recreation center fees, sports fees, and anything else that the family needs that is not always planned, dated or known. I don't always know what my boys will be into next year, or next week! I don't know what school projects are coming this year. I don't know what sports they will play. I don't know the classes or supplies they will need for everything. There are family needs I will need to budget and save for. So we do in our Family Fund.

LIE: Budget's suck. The TRUTH is that Budget's SAVE. They save you from unexpected expenses and emergencies.

SCRIPT: A budget makes my life better.

I love that we have them in our budget every paycheck. They give me peace, comfort, wiggle room and confidence in knowing we have the money and we have the savings to take care of emergencies and our family. That doesn't suck! That feels amazing!

Third, the DEBT. This is where you list the debt from smallest to biggest amount owed, not by the most interest to the least interest owed. We can argue about that all day, but you need to be paying off debt and quickly. You will be energized and keep focused if you see debt go down and get paid off! Listing the smallest debt first will make you pay if off first and you will love the feeling so much you will get intense about the next debt.

If you owe $100 on a debt that has 17% interest, but just keep paying on the highest interest debt of which you owe $3,000 at 29%, you will never pay off the $3,000 fast enough to not earn extra payments due to the interest you are accruing on the $100 bucks! Just pay the $100 bucks off! Just pay the smallest amount due the fastest possible way you can! (Legally:)
SIMPLE MATH PEOPLE!

Credit cards, people you need to pay back, school loans, all of it! Keep your payments going! Keep paying it off! Put your debt in your budget, smallest to largest, making payments and seeing those payments work for you.

Fourth, all the rest of the money. You will have different things than I do listed in our budgets. I have things listed like: School lunches, spa and nails, haircuts, clothing, eating out, entertainment, gifts. Get really specific in your budget about what you are spending and need to spend. Make this budget real for you and your family. Make it flexible, make it work for you.

Do not write the word "SCHOOL" on a line in your budget and then just move on. Write the SPECIFIC school costs. I have "School" listed at the top of a line and then under that I list the specific costs I know: lunches, book fees, bus fees, supplies, teacher gifts, field trip fees. And I keep track of what we spend and what is coming up. I try and know the school costs every month. If something completely unexpected comes up that I did not budget for, I can pull from the Family Fund to cover school expenses. But, I don't have to do that very often because I am specific in that expense.

Do not write the word "FOOD" on a line. That means nothing. That just makes you hungry. Don't be general, be specific. GET SPECIFIC in your budget. You need to write lines under the Food budget stating: Groceries, Eating-Out Lunch, Eating-Out

Dinner, Drive-Thru Coffee, Snacks and Girl Scout Cookies.

The specifics of your food costs and what you want to spend in your budget need to be specifically listed. I hope that helps you to get real and honest about your budget! You will completely see where your money is going and then, you can control it more by making a budget to each line item.

Be careful! When you see that you are actually spending $400 per month on a drive-thru coffee run, it really can't be justified when you can make your own coffee at home for about .42 cents totaling $12.60 per month or less!

Watch out! When you see that you spend $500 per month in clothes and shoes but you can't pay the light bill, and you can easily spend $50 and still look great from consignment boutiques or online retailers, it gets ya!

Be aware! When you see that you are spending $250 per month for Princess to get lunch at school every day, while you bring a sack lunch with peanut butter and jelly, this will cause Princess to argue and have hurt feelings when she learns how to make her own damn lunch!

Line item specific costs and specific goals will give you a clear and specific guide to where your money is going and give you a clear and specific guide to telling your money where to go from now on.

I know you will feel amazing when you write your budget and you will get a real handle on stopping your over-spending.

DAILY DO: Every morning I look at my money. I look at the budget, make certain bills are paid, accounts are full and I know my budget for the day.

My paper bills have a designated place. I labeled a bin area "Pay Bills" and labeled a bin area right next to it "Paid". That is how I organize my paper bills.

My other bills are all paid online automatically every month. You can write them all in an Excel spreadsheet or on a pad of paper. You really need to be paying most of your bills online if possible. It saves you time and energy and money from being "Overdue".

I check all the bills that have been paid online and I mark all the paper bills that have been paid with a really awesome stamp. I purchased my "Paid" stamp from the local business store. For cheap. It's so great and I love marking everything PAID!

When I know my money, I know my budget. When I know my budget, I don't over-spend. PAID!

LIE: Having a budget means I'm broke. Actually, the TRUTH is that having a budget made me rich!

SCRIPT: Living on a budget makes me rich.

Since getting on a budget, I have saved more, paid off all my debt, pay cash for everything and get to keep most of my paycheck. That is not broke. That is loaded!

The lie that you have chosen to believe that budgeting is only for broke people is holding you back from being wealthy. Truly rich!

What wealth may look like to you is different from my view of wealth. I'll sum it up for you how I feel about it. Tell me if you can understand or relate?

"Wealthy" and being "rich" to me is having enough money in the bank that I don't have to worry about anything. My bills are paid, I owe no one, I have no debt and income is still flowing in from many avenues.

My pantry, fridge and freezer are full. My closets are full of clothes and shoes I love. My home is filled with beauty and decorations I love. And my dogs! That is wealthy to me.

My family is together, healthy and we live the life we choose. The homes we own, the cars we drive, the vacations we take. That is wealthy and rich to me. Sitting here, writing in the mountains, with a beautiful view, my family with me, having fun, not a care in the world! That is rich!

Your ideas might be the same, or completely different. But you better figure it out, because lies about budgeting are keeping you poor and broke and over-spending.

What is my idea of being wealthy or rich?

Do I believe that writing and living by a budget is how I get to be rich?
Why or why not?

LIE: A Budget stops me from spending the way I want. The TRUTH is I can spend the way I want because of my budget!

SCRIPT: I live the way I want on a budget.

I tell my money where to go. I tell my money what to do in a budget. If I want to spend money on clothes, I put it into the budget. If I want to spend money at the spa, I put into the budget. I spend the way I want in my budget. I just don't over-spend.

I think the wording for the LIE needs to be re-written: A budget stops me from OVER-spending the way I want. Right? We want, so we spend. We want it now, so we over-spend. So, really a budget stops you from over-spending but that doesn't mean you can't spend the way you want to, you just can't over-spend the way you want to. Am I right?

The truth is, if you don't start living on a budget, your money will be gone and your future will be determined: Working well into your 70's and 80's just to make ends meet.

That is not the future I want for me or my children. A budget-based life allows for you to live a good life today and live a better life in the future. My budget allows for me to spend any way I want, not over-spend any way I want.

Another LIE about living on a budget is that it means I must be living cheap so I look cheap.

Not true! The TRUTH is I look fabulous!

SCRIPT: I don't look cheap, I just buy cheaper.

I never pay full price for anything I wear. I got up early last Saturday to hit a thrift store for .99 cent jeans! I always hit the Clearance racks wherever I go-first! I love consignment and thrift boutiques and I love trading clothes with friends!

My clothes. Just look at my outfit for today. My snow boots, for instance. I got these beauties at a major discount after season last year. Original price for the boots was $149. I purchased them on sale for $29. My skinny jeans are thrift store, $4 bucks. My Columbia sweatshirt was a great find at outlets for $12. No bra today, I'm on vacation. Undies came in a pack of 8, so total $1.50. Cozy socks from a local store on sale for $1.00. Add it up! My clothes cost $18.50 and I will wear them all week! My expensive name brand snow boots only cost me $29! Often, my entire outfits cost less than $20 bucks! And I look great! I just find name brand items for less!

My car. I love it! It's a 2007 Acura MDX. It's paid for. Could I get another one? Yes! But, I love driving a paid-for vehicle and having no car payment is awesome! Is my car a piece of junk? No! Is my car cheap? No! But it was accomplished on a budget.

My home. I love it! It was built in 2010 in Colorado. Could I get another one? Yes! But, I love coming home to this one. It's almost paid off, and we have remodeled it just the way we like it! Is my home a piece of junk? No! Is my home cheap? Not at all! But, we live on a budget.

I don't look cheap, but I buy cheap! That's a budget-based life!

Cool story. So, I really want to paint my bedroom a deep gorgeous rich blue. Just the one wall behind our bed. But, I didn't leave enough wiggle room for paint and supplies in the budget after our vacation. And I don't want to over-spend this week. So, I have been selling items online through Craigslist and Facebook Marketplace locally. I have sold a set of mugs, a floral vase, two home decorations and a set of candles. Together, it's enough for a gallon of paint and a roller brush! Boom! Budget-based living! And I didn't over spend! Now, to paint!

Get on a budget. Do not over-spend. Become truly rich. Love your life. This is good stuff! I hope you are taking notes!

MONEY MANTRA: I want to be wealthy, I want to live a rich life. I can only do that with a budget-based lifestyle.

TOOL #20

STOP SPENDING,
START BRANDING

THERE'S A PRETTY GIRL SERVING AT THE COUNTER
OF A CORNER SHOP
SHE'S BEEN WAITIN BACK THERE, WAITIN FOR HER
DREAM,HER DREAMS WALK IN AND OUT,
THEY NEVER STOP
WELL, SHE'S NOT TOO PROUD, TO CRY OUT LOUD
SHE RUNS TO THE STREET AND SHE SCREAMS
"WHAT ABOUT ME?"
                            -MOVING PICTURES

You have something to offer the world! You just don't know what it is yet. Because you have not taken the time to figure out WHO you are and WHAT you are, you spend all your time spending money. That's why you over-spend.

But you can know who you are and what you are. Start your own personal brand! Stop spending and wasting and instead spend time on getting to know who you are and what you are going to offer the world. Then start branding it!

When I focus my personal self and my professional self on branding, I rock it! I nail it! I own it! I brand it!

"Branding" is a marketing and advertising tool that businesses use to grow sales, grow a market, grow their name big! Business cannot grow without a great brand and great branding campaigns. The Brand is a Name. You are making a personal and professional name for yourself and your side hustle!

You know the brands: Coke, Ford and Home Depot. Do not send me hate-mail if you are a Pepsi Lover, a Chevy Driver or a Lowe's freak. I am simply pointing out that all I have to write is the name and you have a physical, emotional and mental reaction to the brand name because those companies have built a brand over many years. With the name comes the branding.

I personally am addicted to Coke products. Put that sugary bubbly goodness in front of me and it is on! I personally love trucks, but not necessarily the brand. And I could work at Home Depot for the rest of my life if needed and buy everything in that wear house, whether or not I really need that compressor thingy? Who cares? It's just awesome and I would get a discount!

Branding is a message platform, a mapping of sorts for a client or a potential customer. Big business understands this and so should you.

Businesses write and share their stories, compelling stories. The story has characters, challenges, motivations, a setting. Their story has obstacles to overcome, the climax and conclusion.

You have a unique brand story too.

Your life needs a new story! Build your brand and begin a branding campaign!

What might that look like and feel like? Well, I am Jennifer Chase. Wife to Captain Chase, Mom to five boys, Entrepreneur, Philanthropist, Author, Coach, Motivational Speaker, Comedian, Team Leader, Wise Spender, World traveler, Lover of sushi, fine wine, the mountains and the ocean. This is me. I would love to have girls, but boys are my life. My world is full of blue! So, I like to bring some pink in from time to time. That is through girlfriends, spa days and getting my nails done. I know my brand. I am always campaigning! I am always selling it!

I might add or delete anything from that list. Change happens. People happen. Life happens.

But, I remain me, Jennifer Chase. I have a Chase name and brand. My brand includes myself, my family, my life, my work. I have a Frugi brand too. My work branding is about my titles and my actions and making money.

My branding is completed daily through how I live, how I spend my time, how I work it, online media, my writings, my life I live daily. My whole life is a brand. I know exactly who I am. I know my story. I know my name. Do you?

Write at least 10 things that describe your personal Brand?

Who are you? What's your name? Write it out like a business name brand you will live and grow every day!

What do you want your story to be?
How does it end?
It needs to match your branding.

When I open my computer, the main screen has a picture of the ocean. I love that picture, because it represents me so well! I love the beach and I love the sound of the water. It is truly one of my favorite places in the world to be on a beach or near water.

DAILY DO: I also have typed on the same screen, "Our Family Focus: Clarity & Peace, Brightness & Fullness, Fluid & Open, Acceptance & Love."

Those words are our family brand. I can read these words often, daily, many times. It is a constant reminder of my focus, my family's focus, our goals, and any decisions we make during the day need to reflect the brand.

SCRIPT: "I'm not volunteering for that this week. I'm staying focused on this task to complete."

When you keep your focus, you keep your brand, your name, your life moving in the right direction. You stop spending and start branding.

SCRIPT: "I'm sorry, that just doesn't work with my schedule. I'm spending time with my kids that weekend."

You stop making excuses and start making memories.

SCRIPT: "I'm not spending money on that, I don't need it and it doesn't complement my brand."

You stop wondering where your money went and start telling it exactly where to stay.

You stop. You start.

When you design your life like a business brand, watch how you change your money and spending habits. You get serious about building a name for yourself, then you get serious about your money. You begin to watch your time and how it is spent. You have your own business and you didn't even know it!

Money Mantra:

Today, I am building & growing my name brand. Businesses work on a budget. I do too.

TOOL #21

NO MORE VICTIM MENTALITY ONLY AN ABUNDANCE MINDSET

I'LL PUT MY ARMOR ON, SHOW YOU HOW STRONG I AM
I'LL PUT MY ARMOR ON, SHOW YOU THAT I AM
I'M UNSTOPPABLE, I'M A PORSCHE WITH NO BRAKES
I'M INVINCIBLE, I WIN EVERY SINGLE DAY
MIND SO POWERFUL, I DON'T NEED BATTERIES TO PLAY
I'M SO CONFIDENT, I'M UNSTOPPABLE TODAY.
                                          -SIA

There is a thing in this world called a "Cycle of Poverty". Have you ever heard of it? Organizations use the term when discussing people stuck in a constant rut for entire generations of being poor.

As a child, were you poor? Does your family continue to be poor? Do you continue to be poor? If you answered "Yes" to one or more of those questions, you may be stuck in a rut or a cycle of poverty.

Have you really thought about it? Never able to pay the bills? Never able to keep a job? Never able to get ahead? Always asking for help? Always needing support every month?

Need help from the government just to pay your rent, buy groceries, or utilities? Constantly needing help from your parents or friends just to make it? You might be stuck!

Why would you be stuck in a rut of being poor? I mean, it can't feel good, and it can't be peaceful, and who want's to live that way? But you are living that way. Broke. No money. Poor even.

You picked up this book. I know you are looking for answers to your money problems. Over-spending is only part of it. This chapter, this one, gets to the brain of the problem. Ready?

It's your mind. Your brain is wired for living poor. Your mind lives in a constant mindset of victimhood. Poor me. I will always be poor. My parents were poor. My grandparents were poor. I guess, I will be poor too.

Change your mindset from living and thinking poor and instead change your thoughts, your entire mindset on the truth of abundance! ABUNDANCE LIVING!! An abundant mindset will change your entire life.

When you choose to think and breathe abundance, you will find yourself in a great job! You will find yourself in wonderful and loving relationships! You will own your very own car and home. You will have blessings overflowing! When you constantly meditate on the abundance in your life, you sure do open yourself up for more abundance!

When you continue to believe in the big lie of being a victim of poverty, that's what you will continue to live within. Confined in the chains of being poor. Poverty is chains.

Only you can change this. I know that is tough to hear, especially if you are living right now without much. Way to sock a person while their down?!?! Actually, I want to SHOCK you while you're down to wake you up! I want to SHOCK you into believing truth that you were made for more! No one was born to be poor. You were born for purpose. And we ALL have the same exact opportunity to change it. It's our mind. We all have a mind to change our own situation or bless others by helping them change.

SCRIPT: (Victim) "We don't even have enough money to pay rent." (Abundance) "We have the ability to work and make money to pay our rent. I gotta get to work!"

SCRIPT: (Victim) "I never have enough money. I am always broke." (Abundance) "I have worked hard for everything I have right now. I am always blessed and have enough."

SCRIPT: (Victim) "The world owes me. I

have had a hard life." (Abundance) "I can do this on my own! I have what it takes to make it in this world, no matter what it throws at me."

Are you seeing the difference? Can you feel the difference?

No matter your past, no matter your past mistakes, mo matter who has hurt you, no matter the failures, no matter the history of poverty, you can live a life of abundance. I am talking about real abundance! Where you are able to own a home, pay your rent on time, have a vehicle with your own personal name on the title and you own it abundance! I am talking about having money at the end of the month and not living paycheck to paycheck because that's the way you've always done it.

Can you feel the abundance!?!? My DAILY DO in this abundance mindset is to start and end my day with the attitude of gratefulness. Whoops! There is that grateful word again! Being content! Loving what I already have and not being so bogged down with what I don't. Another DAILY DO is that I look at my goal sheet every day. I look at where I am going. I look at how far I have come. I get excited about meeting new goals! I get excited about making money & not over-spending money! I get focused on abundance living. I look at how I will be changing my family tree and changing the cycle of poverty into a cycle of success!

PREEEACHH! Can I get a witness and an Amen?

Michael Hyatt in his book, *Your Best Year Ever*, speaks about gratitude, how this emotion and virtue can change your entire life. He calls it "Gratitude Advantage", explaining how studies have proven how being grateful actually puts you in an advantage point in life for reaching goals, restoring relationships, being successful in all areas of your life just for having a grateful attitude? You can't have an abundant life without having a grateful heart.

Are you continually playing the victim in your life? If yes, what are three ways you can begin to change your mindset habits to abundance thinking and living?

Start with these areas. Choose a few or choose them all! Areas that might be affecting your victim mentality or abundance mindset: Social medias, screen time, your attitude, your type of work, your relationships, negative friends, your sleep patterns, eating patterns, your over-spending habits.

The choice is yours! It's all you baby! Only you can change this. Bummer, right? I mean, it's pretty much your fault. If you continue to live in a victim mentality state, you will remain broke. You will always be in need, want and not grateful. If you learn to live with an abundance mindset, you will learn to live with money, make money, be successful at money.

MONEY MANTRA: I am getting out of the cycle of poverty and living in a cycle of success. Abundance thinking & living out loud!

TOOL #22

STOP THE CONTROLLED CHAOS
START THE COMPLETE ORGANIZATION

So, I started this side hustle called Frugi Organizer. I am invited into people's homes, offices and businesses to help direct them into using systems that are beneficial to them individually, to their company and to their families.

I serve others by getting them organized in any area of their space that is driving them crazy and is their version of controlled chaos.

Why is Frugi Organizer such a hit? Because people and businesses are realizing the benefits of being completely organized. Less mess equals less stress. In organization, they also are finding more time, more money, more happiness. And it feels amazing to be able to find your keys every morning!

I can organize a closet, an entryway, a laundry space. I organize office files, floundering papers, and I even organize failing finances by organizing budgets for clients. I organize kitchen pantries, basements and just about any space that does not bring you joy!

Often, I have repeat business. When I have completely organized one space, I am usually called back to complete another space. It is so honoring that people love my work and I get to serve others, making them happy!

But why would I mention anything about getting organized in a financial coaching book? Because we can talk about not over-spending and I can give you all these tools all day long, but if you are not organized in your finances, in your bill paying system, in your money organization system, in your actions system and if you are not organized in your space, this will not work.

Organized techniques and systems will not only help your home feel wonderful and peaceful in your fung-shui bliss, but having some fung-shui and being organized financially solves many over-spending habits.

Organization allows you to see what you have and what you need. Being organized allows you more time and energy for other important things in your life. Organization habits bring better money habits.

I know us busy-parents like to laugh and joke about our "controlled chaos". But really, there is nothing "controlled" about it. It's just chaos. And it doesn't look good, it doesn't feel good, and it's making me stressed-out just writing about it.

Stop designing your home and your life around chaos and start designing a fulfilling, joyful life around organization and peace.

Find more time, more energy, more rest, more fun by being organized.

Am I living a life in controlled chaos or a life completely organized?

What are 5 things I could do right now to stop the chaos and start living organized?

Here is how I live my life completely organized: Live fearless. I am not afraid of failure, I am not afraid of what others think, I am not afraid of having dirty dishes, I am not afraid of saying No and Hell No to activities, and I am not afraid to work hard and play harder.

I live my life without fear controlling me. What I have found in my Frugi business and in my own life personally, is that when we will live in fear, that is really where the controlled chaos continues. When we let go of fear, that is where true organization can thrive along with our amazing lives!

Some tips on how to live a completely organized life:

1. Stop bringing so much paper into your home. From homework to mail to coupons. **DAILY DO:** I have a trash by our entry door. I go through mail and papers right there. DAILY. It's a great habit. It stops the negative flow of papers into our home. It stops me from spending so much time having to go through papers in my home later.

2. Stop shopping daily. I have mentioned this one before. Love it that much! **DAILY DO:** If you don't shop daily, you don't bring things in daily. Calms the

chaos when you stop bringing it in all the time. I love returning from an event or work and not bringing one damn thing into my home or office. Try it!

3. Stop caring so much what others think. This will help you control your life organized, not chaotically. Your chaos often comes from others? Do you understand the power of people in your life? I sure do! **SCRIPT:** Dump 'em! If certain people are bringing drama and chaos into your home, your office, your family, your life, shut that show down!

4. Stop the belief that living in controlled chaos is okay. It's not. It's a lifestyle. **DAILY DO**: Live in the truth and freedom of a completely organized life. ALL. OF. IT. Home, office, finances, food, work, schedules, business. All of it.

5. Stop hanging on to stuff. It's just stuff. It weighs on your heart and your mind and even your soul. Stuff contributes to a lifestyle of chaos. Stop the hoarding of things that should have been let go years ago. Stop the hoarding of new things to fill an emotional void that does not bring peace. **SCRIPT:** Let it go.

I want you to experience the amazing feeling of not always living in your defined life of chaos. I want you to experience the awesome feeling of always living in your defined organized life. Believe in it, change it, develop it today.

MONEY MANTRA: If I live a life that is completely organized in every area, I truly control a life with no chaos. Being organized controls & changes my spending habits.

TOOL #23

BALLS TO THE WALL!

ALL I DO IS WIN, WIN, WIN NO MATTER WHAT
GOT MONEY ON MY MIND, I CAN NEVER GET ENOUGH
AND EVERY TIME I STEP UP IN THE BUILDING
ALL THE HANDS GO UP, AND THEY STAY THERE, AND
THEY STAY THERE 'CAUSE ALL I DO IS WIN.
                                        -DJ KHALED

Hell to the Ya! Balls to the wall, baby! Load up! Power Up! Wheels Up! Turn and Burn! All aboard! Full speed ahead! All those completely dorky motivational sayings, they get me.

I actually use these in my life. I use all this motivational crap to get me through a tough day, get me through a tough work week, get me through a tough parenting moment. But, I have a lot of success in my personal and professional life and I really think it's because I take this bullshit to heart. Funny right?

I mean, "balls to the wall". Not an endearing saying. Not sure this should be said outside the confines of our homes, but I am telling you, I say this to get my family inspired, on point, ready to go!

Load Up! Power Up! Wheels Up! Right before I go into a new client meeting. It speaks to me and my team, it is time! It is time to do this! It is time to win and there is no going back!

Turn and Burn! All aboard! Full speed ahead! Lots of transportation metaphors right here. I eat them up! Bring it! And I talk in Top-Gun movie lines to my pilot husband and our little men all the time. Most of the time, my husband talks right back to me in Top-Gun movie lines also. That is so sweet! And most of the time, my kids are like, stop it, just stop Mom. We have no idea what you are saying.

Nope! I'm here all week! No autographs please!

If you want to win with money, if you want to truly stop over-spending and change your spending habits, it is time for Balls to the Wall baby! It is time for all in! It is time for the pain and discomfort! It is time for the hard work! It is time for some sweat equity! It is time to stop complaining and start being grateful! It is time to suck it up! It is time to make a mark, a line in the sand! It is time to stop making excuses and start making money$

It is time to put on some lipstick and running shoes and go get it! It is time for balls to the wall and you don't really need any balls but you have a wall and you need to destroy it right now!

You need to go! You need to get this done! You need to save yourself from a lifetime of heartbreak and poverty! You need to pull yourself up out of this debt pit! YOU! You need to control your spending! You gotta find your fire! You gotta get hungry! You gotta want it! You gotta do it! You need to help others and give! You need to live life and love your life!

This isn't a long chapter. This tool is small but BIG VITAL IMPORTANT to the success of your Stop Over-Spending journey. I am so honored that you wanted to walk through it together. I look forward in hearing how you rocked it! Find me on Facebook: Frugi Organizer and on Twitter: @FrugiOrganizer Can't wait to see your badass-balls-to-the-wall win with money!

TOOL #24

GOD

CAN YOU USE THESE TEARS TO PUT OUT THE FIRES
IN MY SOUL, 'CAUSE I NEED YOU HERE
I'VE BEEN SHAKIN, I'VE BEEN BENDIN BACKWARDS
STILL I'M BROKE WATCHING ALL THESE DREAMS GO
UP IN SMOKE
LET BEAUTY COME OUT OF ASHES
AND WHEN I PRAY TO GOD ALL I ASK IS
CAN BEAUTY COME OUT OF ASHES?
                                    -CELINE DION

I may be the only author who ends a chapter with "badass-balls-to-the-wall" and then begins the next chapter with "God".

In my life, I hold the incredible flexible ability to switch from cussing rap music to Jesus worship music in a matter of seconds! I can go from raising my hands in worship listening to beautiful church music to bouncing my head, dancing to Imagine Dragons. Let me explain.

I am not a typical Christian. I need to be honest. I curse like a sailor. I love adult beverages. I listen to rap music and exotic dance music. I don't attend church. I haven't stepped into a church for years or any organized religious ceremony except for the occasional wedding and funeral. I'm taking my three younger boys under the age of thirteen to the Imagine Dragons concert this summer at Red Rocks Amphitheater in Colorado. It's their first concert ever and it is not Jesus music, just awesome music with awesome musicians at one of the most beautiful places in the world.

I don't attend Bible study anymore. I might someday, but not right now. But I still love the Bible. I still study it.

I don't really particularly even like or enjoy religious people anymore. Only a small few who really, truly love people and love God. It is tough when you have a relationship with God but don't fit into the church scene or cliche.

I have been deeply hurt by people who call themselves "Christian" or "religious" or a "church attendee." Those wounds are fresh and scars remain. And that includes my own Christian parents.

My Father works for a Christian organization where the main focus is "family" and yet he hasn't spoken to me, his daughter, in years. My Mother is a radically religious person, yet doesn't have a relationship with her own daughters and grand-children. It's confusing because it is not love. It is not even Christian.

But through all the hurt, through all the rejection, through all that absolute bullshit, I have learned that there is a God who knows me and loves me no matter what. There is a God who cares about me in a way I cannot possibly imagine or comprehend how much He loves me. God is my Father & my Mother. God chooses me.

Have you ever been outcast? Have you ever been the black-sheep? Have you ever been left behind? Have you ever been hurt by someone who attends church every week? Have you ever been divorced? Have you ever cheated on your spouse? Have you ever sinned? Have you ever been a bad parent? Have you ever regretted a decision? Have you ever been terrible at money?
Me too! This is what I have learned and this is what I know.

God loves me, God loves you. No matter who else decides to love you and me. Nor who decides not to. God loves.

No matter my fowl mouth, especially when watching the news! I yell at the T.V. God loves me no matter my failures, my successes, my weakness & strengths. He loves me if I am not a perfect parent, perfect wife, or perfect church attender. He loves me no matter what you think about me. God loves me just as I am. He created me to be just like this and He thinks it is perfect. I do too.

No, I am not typical. But I am typically me. I don't need to attend church every Wednesday and Saturday and Sunday nor do I need to volunteer at church to be considered a "good person". I'm just gonna be me and my relationship with God is between me and Him. It is strong. It is amazing. It is the most important relationship I have.

Oh yes! He is calling me out!

Oh yes! There are things God wants me to focus on, and change and get better at. There is still work to be done. I am a work-in-progress. Can you relate?

Oh yes! There are dreams and ideas God has placed on my heart that will come to fruition. But, it's not what you think. You have no idea what God has placed on my heart and soul. It's between us. And it's really none of your damn business.

Oh yes! God wants me to share all I have to offer to the world. So, I will.

One of the ways I stopped over-spending and being completely out-of-control in my spending habits was developing a great relationship with God. Sounds simple? It is.

One of the ways I found to have a wonderful, intimate, deep, vast, amazing relationship with Him was through His son, Jesus. I highly recommend getting to know this guy.

If you have never accepted Jesus into your heart, I highly recommend it. In fact, I really want to encourage you to open up your heart, mind & soul to Him. Jesus is the best decision I have ever made.

BEST. DECISION. EVER. If you want the best tool to change your habits and to stop your over-spending, a relationship with God and Jesus is the answer. Totally go for it. If you need help on how to ask Jesus into your life, it's really basic and simple. You just say this prayer when you are ready and open to receive His love:

Dear Jesus,

Jen Chase tells me you are pretty amazing. I need help in this money problem I am having and I heard that you can help me. I really need you. I want you to live in my heart, in my soul. I want you to lead me into a better financial situation, one of abundance and peace. Can you help me? I ask that you come into my heart and live there, even if I don't understand, even if I'm

*not the "perfect" Christian. I need help in my
finances. I am out-of-control in my financial life.
I want to be in control of my entire life.
I need you and I am ready for you.
Amen.*

Boom! Done! That's how easy it is. Totally weird that God is a tool for us, right? But, I promise, God and Jesus are real and they are the best tools, the best resources, the best gifts, they are the best new habits I could possibly give you out of everything I wrote for you here in this little book.

God is love. That is all He is, it is all He knows. You need to know His love to stop your over-spending. Accept His love.

Congratulations on your journey, spiritually and physically and emotionally and financially. I love you, friend. If you need help along the way and would appreciate personal coaching in this area, please visit:
www.FrugiOrganizer.com

MONEY MANTRA: I can do this! Grab hold of my life, grab hold to my God, grab hold of my money. Use these tools and make them my new life habits. Stop Over-Spending.

Made in United States
Cleveland, OH
17 May 2025

16996310R00125